THE LITTLE BOOK

ON WEALTH CREATION

AND PRESERVATION

PERSONAL FINANCIAL
MANAGEMENT FOR ALL TIMES

A REALISTIC APPROACH

ELIJAH M. JAMES, PH. D.

Copyright © Elijah M. James

All rights reserved. No part of this book may be reproduced in any form or by any electronic or mechanical means, including information storage and retrieval systems without permission in writing from the author, except by a reviewer, who may quote brief passages in a review.

Canadian Cataloging in Publication Data

James, Elijah M.

The Little Book on Wealth Creation and Preservation: Personal Financial Management for All Times.

ISBN 978-1-7383576-6-6

EJ Publishing

663 White Plains Run

Hammonds Plains

Nova Scotia, Canada B4B 1W7

This book is dedicated to my brother, Marrell (Moriel, for me), for his kindness and support throughout our lives, and to Ms. Koren Norton for her untiring love and devotion. I could not have completed this book without her unflinching support.

Table of Contents

PREFACE 1

ACKNOWLEDGEMENTS 5

CHAPTER 1: INTRODUCTION 6
    The Nature of Money 6
    Functions of Money 7
    Kinds of Money 8
    The Nature of Credit 10
    Kinds of Credit 12
    The Nature of Purchasing Power 14
    Money versus Wealth 14
    Chapter Summary 14

CHAPTER 2: BUDGETING AND RECORD KEEPING 16
    Budgeting 16
    The Cash Budget 17
    Estimating Expenditures 20
    Daily Cash Record 21
    Statement of Assets and Liabilities 23
    Income Tax Records 24
    Other Financial Records 24
    Chapter Summary 24

CHAPTER 3: SAVING 26
    The Importance of Saving 26
    Saving with a Purpose 27

The Power of Compound Interest 28
Saving Vehicles 29
Problems with Saving 32
Conclusions 33
Chapter Summary 33

CHAPTER 4: WISDOM IN SPENDING 35

Spending Involves a Choice 35
A Spending Plan 37
Bargains 38
Timing Purchases 38
Purchasing Considerations 39
Quantity Purchases 40
Buying from Discount Houses 40
Advertising and Labeling 41
Standards and Grades 43
Cash versus Credit Buying 44
Chapter Summary 44

CHAPTER 5: THE VARIETIES OF INVESTMENTS 46

Government Bonds 46
Common Stock 47
Preferred Stock 48
Closely Held and Publicly Held Corporations 48
Corporation Bonds 49
Bond Purchase Considerations 50
Mutual Funds 51
Small Business Investing 52
Real Estate 53

Mortgage Notes and Bonds 54
Chapter Summary 55

CHAPTER 6: THE INVESTMENT DECISION 56

Investing versus Speculating 56
Income, Safety, and Growth 57
Safety of Principal 59
The Dollar-Averaging Principle 60
Income from Investment 61
Marketability of Securities 62
Buying and Selling Securities 62
Chapter Conclusion 63

CHAPTER 7: CREDIT FUNDAMENTALS 64

Importance of Credit 64
Forms of Credit 66
The Charge Account 68
Types of Charge Accounts 69
Credit Terms 70
Credit Cards 71
Cost of Charge Accounts 71
Chapter Summary 72

CHAPTER 8: THE WISE USE OF CREDIT 74

Your Credit Standing 74
Your Line of Credit 76
Credit Rating Agencies 77
Responsibility for Debts 78
Problems with Credit 80

Chapter Summary 80

CHAPTER 9: ELEMENTS OF INSTALLMENT CREDIT . 82

The Nature of Installment Buying 82
Installment Contracts 84
Finance Companies 86
Chapter Summary 87

CHAPTER 10: USING INSTALLMENT CREDIT 88

Buying on the Installment Plan 88
Truth in Lending 93
New Car Financing 95
Finance Charges 95
The Wise Use of Installment Credit 96
Chapter Summary 97

CHAPTER 11: THE CONSUMER AND ADVERTISING 99

Functions of Advertising 100
Criticisms of Advertising 102
Advertising versus Advertising Techniques 103
Kinds of Advertising 105
The Cost of Advertising 106
Consumer Analysis of Advertising 106
Benefits of Advertising 107
Chapter Summary 109

CHAPTER 12: PROTECTION THROUGH INSURANCE 110

The Nature of Property and Liability Insurance 111
Property Insurance 112
Liability Insurance 115

Determinants of the Cost of Property and Liability Insurance.. 117
Automobile Insurance 118
Determinants of the Cost of Automobile Insurance................... 122
Selecting an Insurance Company 123
Chapter Summary 123

CHAPTER 13: LIFE AND HEALTH INSURANCE 124

Meaning of Life Insurance 124
Types of Ordinary Life Insurance... 125
Other Kinds of Life Insurance 128
Characteristics of Life Insurance Policies 130
Health Insurance 133
Chapter Summary 135

CHAPTER 14: BUYING LIFE INSURANCE 137

Selecting an Insurance Company 137
Comparing Costs of Policies... 138
Selecting an Agent 139
Using the Agent 140
Planning a Life Insurance Program 141
Life Insurance Expenditures and Personal Income..................... 142
Insurance as a Source of Future Income 143
Chapter Summary 145

CHAPTER 15: HOUSING THE FAMILY 146

Advantages and Disadvantages of Owning a Home.................... 147
Housing Options 148
Selecting a Home 150
When to Buy a Home 150

Paying for the Home 151
The Buy or Rent Decision 154
Be Cautious in Buying 155
Chapter Summary 155

APPENDIX: GLOSSARY OF FINANCIAL TERMS 157

PREFACE

Following the publication of **Strategic Planning, Budgeting, and Marketing in Small Business Enterprises**, several individuals approached me, not only to congratulate me, but also to press me into further duty. A few of them were small business owners, but many were not; but they all wanted to find out when I would write a book that would help ordinary consumers to survive or even to flourish in difficult economic times. In short, they were asking for a consumer survival kit in an economic crisis.

I thought seriously about the idea and decided that a book that would help consumers, not only in difficult economic and financial times but also in times of normal economic conditions, would be quite useful to large numbers of people. I decided to write *The Little Book on Wealth Creation and Preservation: Personal Financial Management for All Times—A Realistic Approach.*

There is no shortage of books, articles, and blogs that purport to provide instructions and guidelines on how to acquire wealth. Many of them are "get-rich-quick" schemes that are far from realistic and are often on the fringe of illegality. The various forms of "pyramids" and Ponzi schemes come readily to mind. Others require huge investment outlays that only the already wealthy can afford. Still, others involve such a high degree of risk that only the least risk-averse individuals will find them appealing. Following such schemes has too often resulted in financial ruin.

The Little Book on Wealth Creation and Preservation offers a practical and realistic approach to higher standards of living and greater financial and economic security. It takes, as its point of departure, the premise that everyone wants to enjoy a comfortable standard of living. People want to be able to pay their bills, educate their children, buy a home, own a decent car, further their own education, go away on a vacation, and retire without having to significantly reduce their living standards. The purpose of this book is to help people achieve the above economic and financial objectives; thus, the book addresses a wide audience.

Millions of people all over the world deprive themselves of the finer things of life mainly because of a lack of knowledge of money management. Often, the problem is not inadequate income, but poor income management skills. One of the clear messages of this book is that to create and preserve wealth, people must not only *earn* income, but they must also *manage* it.

The book is conveniently divided into 15 Chapters. Chapter 1, the introductory chapter, discusses some fundamental concepts that are necessary for an understanding of wealth creation. It also lays the foundation for the rest of the book. It is safe to say that, except in exceptional cases, such as winning a lottery or coming into an inheritance, wealth creation doesn't just happen; it is planned. Budgeting and record-keeping, the subject matter of Chapter 2, are a part of the wealth planning process. Chapter 3 on saving flows naturally from budgeting, since saving is a prime reason for budgeting.

Chapter 4 discusses wisdom in spending. Spending income wisely is fundamental to achieving and maintaining increased living standards. After practicing wise spending and implementing a successful saving plan, the question is: What next? The answer is: Investing. Chapters 5 and 6 address the investment issue. Whether we like it or not, credit has become an integral part of our economic and financial way of life. Its relationship to wealth creation is undeniable. Chapters 7-10 discuss credit, including credit fundamentals and the wise use of credit and installment credit.

Advertising affects the lives of consumers in many ways. Chapter 11 is devoted to a discussion of advertising and the consumer, while Chapters 12-14 address the issue of consumer protection and insurance.

Life and health insurance are equally important to the process of wealth creation and preservation. With the high and rising cost of health care, life and health insurance assume great significance. These important topics are discussed in Chapters 13 and 14. Chapter 13 can be considered a primer on life and health insurance, while Chapter 14 guides the reader through the process of purchasing life insurance.

Sooner or later, the question of housing the family might emerge as an important issue. Chapter 15 will help with many of the issues surrounding the provision of housing for the family. The fact is, whether the decision is to rent or buy a home, it requires a significant portion of the income.

The glossary of financial terms at the end of the book serves as convenient access to the meanings of specialized vocabulary used in the finance industry.

There can be little doubt that tax considerations have a profound impact on wealth creation and preservation. The omission of taxes from this book is deliberate. Our rationale is that many people do not have too many options when it comes to taxes. The vast majority of those who have options know what those options are and are already taking full advantage of them either directly or indirectly through tax experts.

The Little Book on *Wealth Creation and Preservation* has a prime objective—a mission to help people achieve higher standards of living through better income and resource management. It aims to do so by using a practical and realistic approach.

Who Should Read This Book?

The Little Book on Wealth Creation and Preservation is targeted mainly at people who are interested in a practical guide to the creation and preservation of wealth. This, at once, assumes a wide readership. People who are looking for a "get-rich-quick scheme" will not find much to fancy in this book. In general, the creation of wealth requires dedication and determination. The exposition is simple and direct with no reliance on sophisticated theories and formulas. It is a book mainly for the ordinary reader who is willing to submit to the discipline of adhering to a few practical and common sense guidelines and principles.

ACKNOWLEDGEMENTS

Many people have contributed, in one way or another, to the writing of this book, and I would like to thank them, but they are too numerous to mention all individually by name. A collective "Thank you" is in order. However, there is one person in particular who deserves special mention, and that is the late Dr. Matlub Hussain, who has been a life-long friend and colleague. He read the entire manuscript and made invaluable comments that shaped the final product. I have also benefited much from the comments of many of the participants in my *Money and Financial Management* seminars, and I owe them a debt of gratitude.

Elijah M. James

CHAPTER 1

INTRODUCTION

This book is about money. It's about how to get it, how to spend it wisely, and how to make it grow. This book is also about credit. It's about how you can use credit to your advantage, and how the wise use of credit can help you to acquire wealth. Clearly, money and credit are closely related, but they are not identical. Since money is central to our discussion, let us begin by examining its nature.

> **IS MONEY THE ROOT OF ALL EVIL?**

The Nature of Money

The definition of money is a good starting point. Money can be defined as anything that is generally acceptable as final payment for goods and services or in the settlement of debts. People want money because they can use it to obtain the goods and services that they want. Using money is a convenient way of exchanging goods and services. It is much more convenient and efficient than barter whereby people exchange goods and services directly for other goods and services. The convenience of money is increased because of its availability in amounts as large or as small as necessary. Money can be used to settle a debt of $100,000 or to purchase a 10-cent item.

The notion of general acceptability in our definition of money is significant. Money must be acceptable to those who have things to sell. People are willing to accept money in exchange for goods and services mainly because they, in turn, can use it to obtain the goods and services that they want. When a money item ceases to be acceptable in the process of exchanging goods and services, it will no longer be considered to be money. There is a link between money and wealth. Wealth can be defined as the money value of the things we own. A person who has accumulated a large amount of money is considered wealthy as long as the item used as money can be exchanged for goods and services. If the item used as money ceases to have value and is no longer exchangeable for goods and services, then the person is no longer wealthy.

Functions of Money

Money performs three fundamental economic functions. First, it serves as a medium of exchange; second, it serves as a measure of value; and third, it serves as a store of value. Let us examine each of these functions briefly.

Medium of exchange Money serves as a medium of exchange when people accept it as payment for the goods that they sell, for the various services that they render, and for the labour services that they provide. Money functions as a medium of exchange when we use it to pay for groceries, pay the rent, buy a computer, and when an employer pays us our wages and salaries.

Measure of value Money serves as a measure of value when it is used to give information about the value of things. Distance can be measured in miles and kilometers, and weight can be measured in pounds and kilos. So too, the values of labour services, buildings, or vacation packages can be measured in dollars and cents. A list of prices is an example of money being used as a measure of value, and when we say that a person is worth millions, we are using money as a measure of value. Sometimes, we may not agree with the information that is conveyed when money is used as a measure of value. This is the case, for example, when a customer walks away from an item claiming that it is far too expensive.

Store of value Money is used as a means of storing up purchasing power—the power to purchase goods and services in the future. When you earn income, you may wish to save a part of it for one reason or another. Money placed in savings accounts is performing the store-of-value function. The amount thus saved represents purchasing power that you have earned but have decided to use at some future date. It is a store of value.

Kinds of Money

Money, by which we mean anything that is generally accepted as payment for goods and services, currently exists in three forms:

1. Coins
2. Notes
3. Chequing accounts

Coins

Most people recognize coins as money. They are the metallic money we use for paying very small amounts. They consist of what is commonly referred to as *small change* such as nickels, dimes, quarters, etc. They play an important role in our payments system since they facilitate small purchases and enable us to make change when the amount offered as payment exceeds the value of the purchase.

Typically, the face value of a coin is more than the value of the metal of which it is made.

Notes

Notes are the paper currency with which we are quite familiar. Paper currency is usually issued by the central bank, hence the name "bank notes". The face value of banknotes far exceeds the value of the paper of which they are made. You are willing to offer valuable services for a few pieces of coloured paper (the notes) with face values of $10 and $20 for the simple reason that you, in turn, are able to purchase valuable goods and services using those same pieces of paper.

Chequing Accounts

Chequing accounts are accounts at banks on which you can write cheques. It is important to note that the cheques themselves are not money. Sarah Hughes may accumulate money in a chequing account by depositing notes and coins (currency) in such an account at a bank, she may deposit a cheque paid to her in the account, she may arrange to have her salary deposited directly into the account (direct deposit), or she may borrow money from a bank and have the proceeds credited to her account. In order to pay their bills, many people simply write cheques on their chequing accounts and mail them to their creditors. Today, many people pay their bills online through internet banking. Businesspeople who receive large amounts of cheques usually deposit them in their accounts at banks. This is clearly a matter of great convenience.

Before we leave the discussion of the various kinds of money in common use today, we should mention cash. Sometimes, the term "cash" is used to refer to notes and coins, that is, currency as opposed to cheques. In this book, we use cash to refer to any ready money that an individual or a business actually has, including money on deposit in banks.

A special note on digital money

We must mention a special kind of money that is fast growing in importance—digital currency (cryptocurrency) is a medium of exchange created, stored, and transferred electronically. Although we recognize the existence of this type of money, we will not pay too much attention to it in this book.

The Nature of Credit

Quite simply stated, credit is debt. Whenever cash, goods, or services are provided on a promise to pay at a future date, credit is involved. In our society, most people and organizations use credit in one form or another. The following statement, credited to Earl Wilson, highlights the extent to which we depend on credit:

Modern man drives a mortgaged car over a bond-financed highway on credit-card gas.

Consumer credit is prevalent. It is the basic financial device that most of us use to acquire the things we want when we want them and pay for them out of future income. Therefore, credit represents purchasing power now. Through credit, I can buy a house now, and furnish it now. Through credit, I can buy an expensive car now. Through credit, I can take a Caribbean cruise now; and through credit, I can get married in New Zealand now. A person or a business enterprise has the ability to buy when a promise to pay at some time in the future is acceptable to the seller.

Credit is valuable because it provides purchasing power. Consider this. If individuals, businesses, and governments had to pay cash for everything they buy, business activity would grind to a halt. Of course, to have any value at all, credit has to be acceptable. Credit performs important functions when used wisely.

Functions of Credit

Credit performs the following functions in our society. First, it raises the standard of living. Second, it facilitates business formation; and third, it expands production. Let us discuss each of these functions in turn.

Credit raises the standard of living People can buy houses, automobiles, education, vacations, furniture and appliances, and many other items on credit. This raises their standards of living. Through credit, people can enjoy the good things in life now and pay for them at a future date out of future earnings. Without credit, the number of things that people own would be much less than they currently are with the use of credit.

Credit facilitates business formation Few people today start a new business without using credit. Without credit, many of the businesses we know today would not exist. Manufacturers grant credit to wholesalers who, in turn, grant credit to retailers, who in turn, may grant credit to their customers. Credit keeps the wheels of business spinning smoothly.

Credit expands production Business enterprises can expand the production of goods and services by utilizing credit. They can borrow money to acquire more resources for production. Individuals also may increase their productive capacity by using credit to further their education and training.

Effect of Credit

The use of credit can stimulate the flow of goods and services to consumers. If at least some members of a family are employed with some measure of security of future earnings, the family can buy things now by using credit. Such a family can, through the wise use of credit, plan carefully to meet all debt obligations and enjoy the advantages of a higher standard of living without having cash to actually make the purchases. One rule of thumb worth following is that goods bought on credit should last beyond the time the final payment is made.

Failure on the part of people to meet their financial obligations in terms of credit can result in legal action being taken against them. They can lose their credit standing. Their purchasing power and standard of living will then decrease.

Kinds of Credit

There are many ways of categorizing credit. Credit can be classified on the basis of the specific purpose of the credit. For example, credit categorized as *agricultural* suggests that the credit is extended to farmers. Similarly, a credit that is categorized as *educational* suggests that it is extended for educational purposes. Credit can also be classified on the basis of the source of credit. Thus, the source of a *bank* credit is a bank. A common way to classify credit is on the basis of the borrower and the purpose for which the credit is used. Following this latter classification, we can identify three categories of credit: consumer credit, business credit, and government credit. Let us begin with consumer credit.

Consumer Credit

As the name implies, consumer credit is credit that is extended to consumers to enable them to purchase consumer goods and services on credit. Consumer credit enables many people to purchase the goods and services that they require immediately. Consumers may borrow money from banks to finance expensive repairs on their homes, or to buy cars or other consumer goods and services.

Consumers generally use a type of credit called mortgages to purchase homes. Very few people purchase homes without using credit. Failure to repay the loan as agreed may result in foreclosure and the sale of the property by the lender to get back the money.

Installment buying is popular these days. Under this arrangement, the consumer makes a down payment on the item and agrees to pay the remainder in a given number of months. Credit card use is another extremely popular type of credit. In fact, mainly because of its convenience, many people prefer to buy on credit than to use cash. We will discuss the use of consumer credit further in later chapters. We now turn our attention to business credit.

Business Credit

Business credit, also called commercial credit, is credit that is extended to businesses to facilitate business operations. A furniture manufacturer may order wood, leather, plastic, and other raw materials with a promise to pay its suppliers in 60 days. Similarly, a retailer may stock his or her store with inventories credited from a wholesaler. Farmers may be able to obtain credit with a promise to pay when their crops are harvested. Businesses can also use commercial credit to finance the purchase of buildings, machinery and equipment, and tools.

Government Credit

In the same way that consumers use credit to finance current expenditures, so too, governments borrow money to finance the many projects that they undertake. Tax revenues constitute the main source of income for governments. They often spend more than their current income by using credit. Governments typically borrow money by selling (issuing) bonds. Simply stated, a bond is a certificate of debt with certain features that need not detain us now. Governments borrow money to build schools, highways, airports, nuclear power plants, hospitals, etc. They repay the loans sometime in the future out of future tax revenues.

The Nature of Purchasing Power

The purchasing power of money is defined as the quantity of goods and services that a given amount of money will buy. The quantity of goods and services that a given amount of money will buy depends on the prices of the goods and services. When prices rise, it requires more money to buy the same quantity of goods and services than it did before the increase in prices. When prices rise, the purchasing power of money falls, and when prices fall, the purchasing power of money rises. Clearly, then, the value of money resides in its purchasing power.

Money versus Wealth

Before we end this chapter, we should point out that although money and wealth may be closely related, they are not synonymous terms. This book is about creating and preserving wealth. We discussed money earlier in this chapter so we know what it is. But what exactly is wealth? To answer this question, let us look at a few concepts:

Asset An asset (A) is anything of value that you own

Liability A liability (L) is a debt, something you owe

Net worth or **wealth** (W) is the difference between your assets and liabilities.

$$A - L = W$$

Clearly, anything that increases your assets and reduces your liabilities will help you to create wealth.

Chapter Summary

One can hardly exaggerate the importance of money and credit in our society today. As media of exchange, they are essential to efficient production, and consumption. They play an important role in the attainment of personal happiness and security. They are vital elements in the acquisition of wealth. In the absence of money and credit, the standards of living now enjoyed by many people would not have been possible. It is mainly by the wise use of money and credit that individuals will acquire and preserve wealth.

CHAPTER 2

BUDGETING AND RECORD KEEPING

Financial planning is at the very heart of wealth creation. If you have never engaged in any financial planning, it might be a reason why you have not been able to accomplish your financial goals. Many people do not practice any serious financial planning because

> YOUR BUDGET IS YOUR FINANCIAL PLAN

they don't know how. In this chapter, we will follow some simple but important steps in financial planning. Financial planning involves budgeting, record keeping, and making provision for saving.

Budgeting

A budget is a document that outlines estimated or planned revenues and expenditures of an economic entity (individual, family, business, government) for a period of time. It is a systematic plan for using available resources to accomplish financial objectives. Budgeting is the process of developing such a plan. Functioning without a budget of some kind is analogous to trying to sail a ship without a rudder. You will end up somewhere, but not necessarily where you want to go. Budgeting involves the following two activities:

a) Estimating the amount of money that will be available for the period
b) Planning the expenditures for the period.

In budgeting, income and expenditures are significant factors. Income includes not only money received in wages and salaries, but also any profits from business operations, interest earned on savings, dividends earned on shares, and earnings from other sources. Not all the income earned as wages and salaries is available for use because income taxes must be deducted. The amount of cash available can be determined by adding together the following items: (a) the cash available at the beginning of the period, (b) estimated income, and (c) any loans.

For budgeting, expenditures include not only actual money spent on items that will be used up, but also money spent on items that will last a long time, and the placing of money into savings and investments. Payments on homes and loan repayments must also be included in expenditures.

The Cash Budget

A simple method for setting up a cash budget can be easily illustrated. Look at the monthly cash budget illustrated in Table 2.1 below. The budget column at the far right contains estimated figures for the month. The column just before it lists the actual cash available and actual expenditures for the month. The actual figures are obtained from events and transactions during the month. The sources of the actual figures will be discussed later. Notice that provision is made to list cash available to be spent. Cash available includes actual cash on hand or in chequing accounts, expected income, and any borrowed funds. Savings put away for emergencies and special purposes are not included in cash available for budgeting purposes. If however, you expect to draw on those savings for expenditures, then those amounts should be included in the cash budget.

Table 2.1
Monthly Cash Budget of Income and Expenditures

Month_____

Item	Actual ($)	Budget ($)
Cash available:		
Salary or wages	3,000.00	3,000.00
Interest & dividend	Nil	Nil
Borrowed funds	Nil	Nil
Other: (Specify)	Nil	Nil
Total cash available	3,000.00	3,000.00
Fixed expenses:		
Donations	350.00	350.00
Rent/mortgage	800.00	800.00
Auto insurance	440.00	450.00
Real estate taxes	60.00	75.00
Payments on debts	35.00	40.00
Total fixed expenses	1,685.00	1,715.00
Variable expenses:		
Water, heat & telephone	120.00*	75.00
Internet	40.00	40.00
Electricity	40.00*	30.00
Groceries and housekeeping materials	540.00*	500.00
Clothing	60.00*	50.00
Transportation/gasoline	260.00*	230.00
Recreation & education	100.00*	90.00
Personal & toiletry	55.00*	30.00

Item	Actual ($)	Budget ($)
Medical & dental	---	---
Other (specify): Miscellaneous	75.00*	40.00
Total variable expenses	1,290.00	1,085.00
Summary		
Total cash available	3,000.00	3,000.00
Total expenses (fixed & variable)	2,975.00	2,800.00
Amount available to save and invest	25.00	200.00

The pertinent month should be written in the space provided at the far right at the top of the table. Bear in mind that we are focusing here on cash available. Funds deducted from your pay (payroll deductions) are not available to you for spending. For this reason, we shall consider only your net wages (your take-home pay) when estimating cash available. Wages and salaries can be estimated quite closely by considering wages and salaries in the past and by making any adjustments that you may anticipate because of wage increases or decreases or because of any expected overtime or unemployment. In Table 2.1, wages and salaries are estimated at $3,000.00 for the month under consideration.

Interest and dividend payments received should also be included in cash available. An easy way to estimate these is to assume that they will be the same as in the immediate past. For the month under consideration, interest and dividends received were zero. Sometimes it is necessary to borrow money. When this happens, the borrowed money becomes part of the cash available to spend. There was no borrowed money for the month being considered. When borrowed money is repaid, it is recorded as an expenditure item.

Estimating Expenditures

You will notice from Table 2.1 that there are two categories of expenditures: fixed expenditures and variable expenditures. In estimating your expenditures, record first those payments that you know have to be made. These are the *fixed payments*, many of which represent large expenditures. For example, you know that you have to pay the rent if you are a tenant, and you know you have your mortgage payment if you have purchased a home and have a mortgage.

You may have certain insurance policies and will know in advance when the payments are due and how much they are. It is probably a good practice to include savings in the category of fixed payments. In this way, saving becomes a planned activity. If you do not plan your savings in advance, before you allow money for the many optional items, you will probably never save any money. In any event, saving must be a conscious activity. As a matter of habit, some people take out of each pay cheque the amount they want to save. In this discussion, we assume that the individual plans to save $200 each month. Before we leave the subject of fixed expenditures, you should note that payments on money borrowed, interest on loans, and installment payments that come due should all be included under this classification.

The *variable payments*, those that are smaller in amounts or more subject to change, may be estimated on the basis of past experience but adjusted to suit anticipated needs. Water, heat, electricity, gas, and telephone are included in the variable payments category. You will notice that many of these payments are relatively small. An important consideration in setting up your budget is deciding whether you spent too much last year or whether you will have to spend more. Often, this decision is a judgment call. If food prices have gone up, you may decide that you need to spend more on this item. If one child has graduated from school and will be working at a full-time job soon, you can budget less for school expenses. If you are planning a paint job for the car, you should include the amount in you budget.

Daily Cash Record

Notice the cash record shown below in Table 2.2. It contains a column for the actual cash available and one for the actual expenditures for each month. However, you will observe that there is only one line for each item in the columns. Several times during the month you may receive wages and purchase groceries and other items. It is necessary, therefore, to keep a continuous daily record of all types of cash income and expenditures so that these amounts can be summarized at the end of the month and then recorded in the proper columns in the budget.

Table 2.2
Daily Record of Expenses

Month_____

Date	Particulars	Amount
May 1	Breakfast at cafeteria	$ 5.00
May 1	Tea at Fresh Cup (2 cups)	5.00
May 1	Lunch with Peter	35.00
May 1	Groceries	80.00
May 2	Newspapers	4.00
May 2	Lunch	11.50
May 2	Blue dress	17.50
May 2	Gasoline	45.00
May 3	Breakfast	6.00
May 3	Snack with soft drink	6.50
May 3	Lunch	15.50
May 3	Video rental	5.00
May 4	Breakfast	4.50
May 4	Lunch	16.50
May 4	Telephone	35.00

Date	Particulars	Amount
May 4	Electricity	25.00
May 5	Lunch	6.50
	Total Expenses for Month	$2,975.00

The table shows only a partial picture of the expenditure activities for the entire month. At the end of the month, the amounts are totaled and carried to the appropriate row in the first column of Table 2.2. For the month of May, the amount is $2,975.00. But the total cash available is $3,000.00. Therefore, the amount available to save and invest is only $25.00. The plan to save $200.00 cannot be realized.

You can remedy the deficiency in planned savings by increasing cash available, by reducing expenditures, or by some combination of both. In practice, increasing cash available is difficult. It might not be a simple matter to increase wages or salary, or interest and dividends; and it may not be wise to borrow funds, the financial obligations of which might prove to be burdensome. Similarly, the fixed expenses are often not subject to manipulation. Therefore, it is the variable expenses over which you have the most control. The items that need attention so that you can achieve your saving objective are marked with an asterisk (*) in Table 2.1. Only the internet expense was on target.

You can reduce your variable expenses by:

1) reducing expenses on water, heat, and telephone (reduce water use, turn down the heat, and reduce long-distance calls);
2) Using less electricity (turn off unnecessary lights, use more energy-saving devices, and switch to compact fluorescent light (CFL);
3) Purchasing cheaper but nutritious groceries;
4) Eliminating unnecessary purchases of clothes;

5) Reducing transportation costs (make fewer trips by car, if possible);
6) Reducing expenditures on recreation and education, if possible;
7) Purchasing fewer or less expensive personal and toiletry items; and
8) Eliminating impulse buying.

Statement of Assets and Liabilities

Let us begin this section by defining the terms *asset* and *liability*. An asset is anything of value that someone owns. A liability is a debt that is owed to someone. It is quite useful in the wealth acquisition process to determine how much is owned and how much is owed. A statement of assets and liabilities, also called a *balance sheet*, will show what the real net worth is. The net worth or capital is the difference between total assets and total liabilities.

Table 2.3 illustrates a simple balance sheet for a family. For this purpose, the family had to estimate the value of household furniture and appliances.

Table 2.3
Balance Sheet for a Hypothetical Family
December 31, 20___

Assets ($)	Liabilities ($)
Cash in chequing account 800.00	Loan 10,000.00
Cash in savings account 900.00	Credit card debt 2,500.00
Savings bonds 1,000.00	**Total liabilities 12,500.00**
Household furniture 6,000.00	Net worth (18,700 − 12,500.00) =
Appliances 2,000.00	6,200.00
Automobile 8,000.00	**Total liabilities**
Total assets 18,700.00	**& net worth 18,700.00**

Income Tax Records

The government requires its citizens to pay income taxes. Therefore, in addition to the records needed for the cash budget and the statement of assets and liabilities, you will also need to collect some information during the year that will help you fill out your income tax return. This will help you to claim certain legitimate deductions.

In many countries, each employer is required to provide each employee with a statement indicating the amount of income tax withheld. To be able to claim certain deductions, you may be asked to provide proof of having paid such expenses. It is therefore wise to keep canceled cheques and receipts for such payments.

Other Financial Records

A record of valuable items such as furniture, appliances, books, jewelry, silverware, and valuable collectibles such as rare stamps and coins should be kept to provide an inventory in case of loss by fire or theft. Dates of purchase, from whom acquired, and prices should be indicated on the record. Some insurance companies provide a form on which such items can be recorded. In addition, deeds of property, stock certificates, bonds, and insurance policies should be recorded and kept in a safe place such as a safe deposit box.

Chapter Summary

Budgeting and record-keeping, key elements in financial planning, are major planks en route to wealth acquisition and maintenance. Success is much less likely without them. A cash budget and a daily cash record will help you to manage your finances so that you can better achieve your financial objectives. Controlling your expenses is crucial to acquiring and maintaining wealth. Knowing what you own and what you owe is important because the difference between the two is what you are worth financially. A balance sheet captures this information.

CHAPTER 3

SAVING

In Chapter 2 when we discussed budgeting, we noted that a budget should include regular amounts for savings. Unless savings are planned and a conscientious effort is made to implement the plan, there usually will be no savings.

SAVING IS ONE OF THE KEYS TO FINANCIAL SUCCESS

Without savings, you are unlikely to obtain many of the really important things you want to improve your living standard.

The Importance of Saving

When the inhabitants of a country save, their collective accumulation of savings can be used for business financing, thus creating new capital, new jobs, and greater production of goods and services for the benefit of all. Therefore, as you save and put your money where it can earn interest, you are helping not only your country but also yourself.

Saving involves setting aside a part of income regularly. A regular plan of saving is viewed as evidence of good money management. Saving can be enjoyable if you look forward to some greater future pleasures by giving up some of your present spending for unwise or unnecessary things. An important question is whether you are willing to make and implement a plan that will enable you to achieve a desirable and pleasant objective.

Saving with a Purpose

It is probably safe to say that most people have some definite goals in life—some things toward which they are striving. Some of these goals are really ideals and ambitions, and some are desires and wishes for material things that add to the comfort and pleasantness of living. Some people may not be interested in amassing great fortunes, but they do want a pleasant life. They want to be able to pay their bills when they become due, take an occasional vacation, own a car, educate their children, etc. Regardless of the kind of goals that you may set for yourself and your family, money is usually a key factor in achieving them. Most people have to set aside a little at a time from their income in order to accumulate enough to realize their goals.

People save for a variety of purposes. Usually, the more important the reason for saving is, the stronger will be the incentive to save. Some popular goals/reasons for saving are:

- To buy a car
- To take a vacation
- To leave an inheritance
- To start a business
- To provide for or to further one's education
- To purchase a home
- To retire comfortably
- To provide for emergencies
- To get married

- To make donations to a church or charity
- To purchase furniture and appliances
- To invest
- To have security and safety
- To have financial freedom

The Power of Compound Interest

Perhaps there are not many people who fully understand the cumulative power of compound interest. It is mainly through this device that your savings will grow and one of the ways through which your money will work for you. However, although interest is a very faithful servant, it can work for you only if you have savings. Many people are able to enjoy a comfortable standard of living even after they retire largely because of the miracle of interest. Although they no longer work, their money continues to work for them, earning interest year after year.

For example, if you deposit $5,000.00 in a savings account that pays interest at the rate of 5% twice a year, after five years, your $5,000.00 will grow to $6,400.42. In ten years, it will grow to $8,193.08. Let us see how a saving plan of $200 a month will perform. Table 3.1 shows how much will be accumulated if a sum of $200.00 is deposited each month in a savings account at various rates of interest. We assume that interest is computed semiannually. For example, if you start saving $200 a month now, and if the interest is computed semiannually at 5% a year, you would have $31,419.92 in ten years, which you could use towards the down payment on a home.

Table 3.1 Growth of Savings

Amount of savings					
At end of	Annual rate of interest				
	2%	2.5%	4%	4.5%	5%
5 years	$12,680.00	12,856.72	13,402.46	13,589.90	13,780.16
7 years	18,116.28	18,463.60	19,552.10	19,931.02	20,318.32
10 years	26,687.04	27,414.02	29,739.98	30,566.44	31,419.92
15 years	42,159.28	43,896.82	49,655.32	51,773.58	54,000.32
20 years	59,250.28	62,559.82	73,932.02	78,265.64	82,905.14

Clearly, the higher the rate of interest, the greater will be the amount after any given period. Interest rates are neither consistently high nor consistently low. In the next section, we discuss where you can put your savings.

Saving Vehicles

Most individuals are able to save only a few dollars each month. Hence, like many other people, you need a place to put your monthly savings until a sufficient amount accumulates to enable you to invest in bonds, stocks, real estate, or in some other form of permanent investment. Below are some places where you can place your savings. In deciding upon a saving vehicle, you should consider the following:

1. Will your savings to safe?
2. Will the funds be available at any time?
3. Will the funds earn a reasonable rate of interest?
4. How often is interest compounded?

Commercial Banks

Commercial banks, through their savings department, accept savings deposits. They are usually conveniently located, making it easy to deposit savings at the time of cashing or depositing a pay cheque. The interest on savings may be credited annually or semi-annually. Some banks require notice before you can withdraw funds from a savings account, especially when the withdrawal is substantial. This right is quite often not exercised, but it may be exercised if necessary. Time deposits usually earn a slightly higher rate of interest than do regular savings accounts. A time deposit may be made for a period of six months, one year, or longer; and the bank issues a certificate to the depositor indicating that the deposit, plus interest at the agreed rate, may be withdrawn at the end of the specified time. A minimum amount of money, such as $1,000.00 is required in order to purchase certificates of deposits (CDs). It is important to note that deposits in commercial banks are insured up to a stipulated amount. The Federal Deposit Insurance Corporation (FDIC) in the United States, the Canada Deposit Insurance Corporation (CDIC) in Canada, and the Financial Services Compensation Scheme (FSCS) in the United Kingdom each insures each deposit account in the respective country to the extent of a given amount.

Savings Banks

A savings bank is a financial institution established with the main purpose of accepting savings deposits from the public. Funds deposited in savings accounts on savings banks earn interest. Like commercial banks, savings banks may grant loans to businesses and consumers. Like commercial banks, savings banks also accept time deposits in addition to regular savings deposits.

Savings and Loan Associations

Savings and loan associations are organized for the purpose of lending money to people who do not have enough money to buy or to build a home. The funds lent by the association are accumulated from depositors. In many cases, when people make deposits in a savings and loan association, they actually buy shares and become part owners. These shares earn income generally at a slightly higher rate of interest than that on a regular savings account in a commercial bank or a savings bank.

Savings and loans associations will also accept time deposits at a slightly higher rate of interest or dividend than is generally paid on demand deposits (deposits that do not require notice prior to withdrawal). In this regard, the practice is similar to that of savings departments of commercial banks. Normally, withdrawals may be made from savings and loan associations without prior notice. However, in most cases, the institution is allowed some time (usually 30 days) to fill a request for a withdrawal. In times of economic stress, additional legal restrictions may be imposed for the protection of the institution and the depositor.

Government Savings Bonds

Government savings bonds such as United States Savings Bonds in the United States, Canada Savings Bonds in Canada, and British Savings Bonds in the United Kingdom are relatively good savings vehicles. These bonds can be purchased from commercial banks and other financial institutions in various denominations. While the rate of interest on government savings bonds may not be high, it is reasonable in comparison with the rate of earnings on some other savings, and purchasing government savings bonds is quite safe.

Credit Unions

Credit unions, popular in many countries, are cooperative associations operating both as savings and as lending institutions for the benefit of their members. Credit unions are usually formed by large groups of people with common interests. They may be formed by groups such as teachers, workers in large factories, and members of churches. Members of credit unions receive dividends representing interest earned on the funds deposited with the credit unions and lent to others.

Endowment Insurance

You will learn more about life insurance in a later chapter. Most life insurance policies provide not only protection but also savings. Endowment insurance is a type of life insurance that is payable to the insured if he or she is still alive on the maturity date of the policy, or to a designated beneficiary if the insured is not living. Endowment insurance policies combine life insurance with a high degree of savings. An endowment policy is purchased over a stated number of years, such as 10, 20, or 30. The cash value of such policies builds up rather rapidly. Many people use endowment policies as a combination of protection for the family while saving for some specific purpose.

Annuities

Life insurance annuities are another means of saving. An annuity is a contract that is sold by an insurance company with the purpose of providing payments to the holder at specified intervals, usually after retirement. If you have a certain sum of money, such as $5,000.00, you can use it to purchase a life insurance annuity, which at a stipulated age will be paid back to you in monthly payments with interest. Many people include an annuity as a part of their retirement plan.

Problems with Saving

There is some element of risk in any saving plan. You can reduce this risk by making sure that your savings are safely placed. Interest rates may change from time to time. When they fall, your interest income will also fall, other things being equal. Also, the amount of dividends declared may vary, depending on economic conditions. For example, if banks find themselves in a position where they have more money than they can lend or invest profitably, they will tend to reduce the interest rates they pay on funds deposited with them.

Another problem exists with saving. Suppose you have $10,000.00 in a savings account on which you are drawing interest. If prices in general rise persistently over a ten-year period – a situation referred to as inflation, the purchasing power of your savings will be eroded away by the higher prices of goods and services. If the annual rate of inflation is sufficiently high, the real value or purchasing power of your savings will actually diminish. That is what is meant when it is said that people with savings lose during inflationary times.

Conclusions

Several important conclusions can be drawn from the discussion about saving. Let us summarize them here.

1. You have to decide whether to spend now or save in order to be able to enjoy a higher standard of living in the future.
2. A budget is a key element in any meaningful savings plan.
3. You should establish goals for saving since goals tend to motivate you to save.
4. It makes sense to set aside even small amounts each month as savings. The power of compound interest will increase savings of even small amounts.
5. There are several relatively safe saving vehicles.

Chapter Summary

If you want to acquire and preserve wealth, you have to save. Putting aside a part of your income each month helps to build wealth. Saving is important because it enables you to enjoy a higher standard of living in the future. People save for a variety of reasons—to pay for a wedding, to purchase a car, to take a vacation, to educate children, etc. through the power of compound interest, a given sum of money will grow appreciably. Saving vehicles include commercial banks, savings banks, savings and loan associations, credit unions, and government savings bonds. Falling interest rates and inflation negatively affect savings.

CHAPTER 4

WISDOM IN SPENDING

Creating wealth is not only a matter of earning money, but it is also about wisdom in spending. You probably know people who earn huge amounts of money and yet are heavily in debt.

LIVE WITHIN YOUR MEANS

You probably also know people with smaller incomes who somehow manage to save money and create wealth. The difference is in spending habits. In this chapter, you will learn some important guides for spending money. The following quote is attributed to Will Rogers:

"Too many people spend money they haven't earned to buy things they don't want to impress people they don't like."

Spending Involves a Choice

Buying is always a matter of making choices. Choices must be made between:

a) spending your money now or saving it for future use
b) wants and needs

c) one product and another of the same kind
d) two entirely different kinds of products.

It is not worth buying something unless it is worth more to you than the money you spend on it. If you take the time to think carefully about every purchase that you make, there is less chance that unneeded and unwanted luxuries will be purchased under high-pressure advertising and selling in preference to satisfying the real needs of the family. In this post-modern society where present gratification is predominant, the tendency towards current consumption is strong. Before every purchase, you should ask yourself the following four questions:

1. Do I really need to make this purchase? If so, why?
2. Is it worth the cost in terms of my effort to earn the money?
3. Can the money be put to better use?
4. Am I buying this item just to follow others? To make a statement? To draw attention to myself? To make someone envious?

In a very real sense, the real needs of the average family in a developed country such as the United States, Canada, the United Kingdom, and Australia are relatively limited but wants can be increased almost without limits. As a result of high-pressure advertising and hard selling and our rising levels of living, a tendency exists on the part of many people to want to "keep up with the Joneses" and to justify in their own minds that what really is a luxury is actually an urgent necessity.

The vast majority of families do not earn enough money to enjoy unlimited purchases of luxuries. On the contrary, many families cannot afford to purchase all their real needs without very strict self-restraint in making their purchases. This is one reason for the importance of a budget. In many families, the tendency is to follow individual selfish urges in satisfying emotional wants rather than practicing individual self-restraint for the benefit of the entire family. If mother wants something, she may buy it on an emotional impulse; if father wants something, he buys it without consulting the family; if the children want something, and they have their own money, they spend it without much thought, or they exert pressure on parents to obtain the things they want. Most families can get the most out of their income if family purchasing is considered from the point of view of unselfish needs.

Even in the case of small purchases, a great amount of money can slip through the fingers of every member of the family in buying little things called *impulse items*. They are the little things in the nature of luxuries that sit by the cash register and are easy to pick up for $2.99 or even more, just on an impulse because the buyer may have a little money in his or her pocket, wallet, or purse.

A Spending Plan

There are not many people who earn so much money that they can buy all they want without considering whether they have enough money to pay for their purchases. Therefore, a spending plan is necessary. Although budgeting was discussed earlier in this book, it is desirable to review it at this juncture because of its relationship to buying. Recall that a budget is a plan of spending and saving. The plan will help you to determine how much to spend and how much to save. When the spending program is broken down into months and weeks, it should be checked periodically with the original plan to be sure that overspending is not taking place. The plan must often be revised and adjusted to take care of unforeseen problems as they arise. In other words, the plan must be flexible.

A spending plan has the following distinct advantages.

1. It helps you to live within your means.
2. It helps you to save so that you can create wealth.
3. It reduces impulsive and reckless spending so that you can focus on buying the things that you really need.

Bargains

At some point or another, most retail stores have special sales during which prices are lower than at other times. Some sales include standard items that are kept in stock regularly. Other sales are clearance sales to close out styles, models, or items at the end of the season. Some are sales of special goods brought in for the sale.

In almost every community, a pattern can be observed yearly by most stores, such as sales of housewares in March, school clothes in August, furniture in August, and toys after Christmas. You can find bargains and save money by waiting for sales.

Timing Purchases

The previous brief discussion indicates some types of sales in which you can often purchase at bargain prices. This is especially true when merchants sell their regular merchandise at reduced prices. However, some merchants bring in special merchandise for special sales and do not reduce the price of their regular merchandise. Some of the special merchandise may be good, but it is wise to compare it with the regular merchandise that the store normally sells. The following is a list of examples of bargain sales:

1. Remnant sales of merchandise of odd lengths, sizes, and assortments.
2. Sales of soiled goods that may be returned goods, shopworn goods, or sample merchandise.
3. Pre-season sales in advance of the regular season.
4. Pre-inventory sales to reduce stock of merchandise on hand.
5. Out-of-season sales of merchandise left over at the end of a season.
6. Odd-lot sales of merchandise, such as irregulars or seconds.

7. Surplus stock sales resulting from overbuying of a merchant or over-production of a factory.
8. Anniversary sales as a special event to stimulate business.
9. Special seasonal sales that offer bargains in season.

At the beginning of a season, style goods sell at their highest prices. As the season progresses, the prices are gradually lowered, for merchants hope to dispose of their goods before the end of the season.

For obvious reasons, fresh fruits and vegetables usually sell at their cheapest prices during the summer. As one might expect, products that are most difficult to store have wide fluctuations in price. The prices of canned goods tend to be lower soon after the canning season.

Particularly during periods of generally high and rising prices, you should avoid buying anything that you do not absolutely need. You should save your money and wait until prices are lower. Of course, families have to eat regularly. Purchases of food cannot be long deferred until prices fall. However, you can watch prices and buy the kinds of foods that are currently being sold at the most attractive prices.

Purchasing Considerations

There are two extremes of thinking as far as prices are concerned. One is that the highest-priced item is the best; the other is that the lowest-priced item is the best bargain. Neither perspective is necessarily correct. The price of an item must be related to its quality, its economy, and how it satisfies your needs and wants.

Many things determine quality for different people. For some people, beauty is what they want; for others, long-wearing economy is sought; still others want special features, such as a timer on a stove.

What is quality? It may be many things to many people, but in general, it is a combination of design, colour, workmanship, beauty, wearing quality, and economy. On the other hand, the best bargain may be the product that is the best buy for the money. It could be the cheapest, or it might be the highest priced.

Price may not be the most important consideration in buying, even when buying the same product or brand of product. In all cases of buying mechanical or electrical equipment, as well as many other products, the main consideration is to obtain a product that will operate without trouble, but when trouble occurs, you can get good repair service. Make sure that you get a product that will wear well, and above all, one that you can get repaired when this service is needed.

Quantity Purchases

Because of possible quantity discounts, people who buy in the smallest units usually pay more than those who buy in larger units. For example, an eight-ounce can might sell for $2.00, but a 16-ounce can of the same thing may sell for $2.80. Besides buying in larger units, if they are needed, it is often possible to buy more units at a reduced price. For example, one unit might sell for $3.00; two for $5.40; and three for $7.50. But buying more than is needed or a larger size than can be consumed without waste is not economical.

Buying from Discount Houses

In many countries, there are establishments commonly known as *discount houses* that attempt to sell merchandise at prices lower than those of anyone else. Generally, discount houses operate in the fields of household equipment and appliances, but they may also operate in clothing and other fields. Sometimes these firms sell standard merchandise like that sold in other stores, but very often they sell unknown brands. Some of the brands may be good, but others may be of questionable quality. A discount house attempts to sell a great deal of merchandise at a low margin of profit in the hope that there will be a large total profit on the operations.

If you buy a household appliance from a discount house, you may find it necessary to obtain service from an independent repair service provider. However, if you buy a piece of equipment made by a nationally known company with a local service organization, you can obtain service and repair parts from the local service agency of the manufacturer. On some products, you may be able to obtain the same guarantee from a discount house as from any other store; but in purchasing from a discount house, you should assure yourself that you are getting good merchandise.

Advertising and Labeling

Advertising

You, as a consumer, can benefit from advertising; but in order for advertising to be of value to you, you must know how to use it wisely. Advertisements should be analyzed from two perspectives:

 a) for information about the product, and
 b) for deceptive or misleading statements.

Some advertisements are neither informative nor deceptive. They are simply evasive or general, or they merely appeal to the emotions. The intelligent consumer will look for helpful information. You should learn to distinguish between emotional appeals and rational appeals. You should learn to evaluate testimonials and to discern the facts that are included.

From a consumer's perspective, an advertisement may be considered primarily good if it provides facts about the quality, standards, specifications, performance, and uses. It cannot be considered good for the consumer if it fails to provide this information and instead appeals only to the emotions. Here are some questions that you can ask in analyzing advertisements.

 1. Do I need the item that is advertised?

2. Is the product beneficial?
3. What does the product contain and how is it made?
4. How economical is the product?
5. How long will the product last?
6. How does its price compare with the prices of similar products?
7. Does the item carry any seals identifying its quality or any evidence of authoritative scientific tests?
8. Is there any proof to back up the assertions?
9. Are there any service or maintenance problems?
10. Are any of the advertising statements evasive or misleading?
11. Does the advertisement appeal to your intelligence?
12. Does the advertisement make you feel confident that, if you buy, you will be a satisfied customer?

Labeling

In the long past when practically all food, clothing, and other necessities were prepared and made in the home, there was little need for standards and grades. Consumers purchased raw materials from which to make the things they needed. Processed goods and ready-made clothes were practically unknown. Purchasers could see what they were buying and in some instances, they even tasted the food before they bought it. There were few choices to make, for usually the merchant had available for sale only one kind of tea, shoes, or furniture.

Today, when most of the food, drugs, clothing, and other things we buy are finished products and ready to be used, merchants keep in stock a variety of each kind of commodity from which we choose the one that appeals to us. Many commodities, such as food and drugs, are in cans or otherwise packaged so that we do not actually see them until we use them. Standards and grades thus are very important to modern consumers. Standards indicate to us what the commodity really is, what it is made of, and what its characteristics are. If there are several qualities of a commodity, such as there are in foods, grades indicate the level of the quality.

A label is a written statement attached to an article or a commodity describing its essential characteristics. Standards and grades, as well as other information of importance to consumers, may be indicated on the label. You should familiarize yourself with standards and grades; you should carefully read the labels on merchandise to learn the characteristics of the goods that you are contemplating buying.

In examining a label, you should look for the following information:

1. Specific descriptive statements.
2. Facts regarding quantity.
3. Facts regarding quality.
4. Grades or other similar designations.
5. Certificate or other mark of approval or guarantee.
6. How to use and care for it.
7. Warnings.

Standards and Grades

Simply stated, a standard is a unit of measure. A kilo is a measure of weight; a meter or a foot is a measure of length; and a gallon or a liter is a measure of liquids. Without these standards of quantity, it would be difficult or impossible to purchase sugar, fabric, flour, or milk. Without such standards, how could prices be set? How could you indicate how much of a commodity you want? It would be practically impossible.

Standards of quantity are not the only standards. We designate the size of a pair of shoes by length and width; the size of a shirt by neckband size and sleeve length; and some articles, such as hats and sometimes dresses, by arbitrary numbers. Other kinds of standards pertain to performance, such as the octane rating of gasoline or the heat units, known as British Thermal Units (BTU) in coal.

A standard ordinarily is thought of as a measure of quantity, weight, or extent, and sometimes of quality. A standard for consumer goods is usually a definition that states fully what the yardstick is.

With the exception of food, standards usually define a single level of quality of a commodity that is considered satisfactory. A drug, for example, either complies with some official formula, or it does not. There are no degrees of conformance to the drug standard. But when applied to foods, standards often are established to define several levels of quality, each of which is known as a grade. For example, there are different grades of eggs. A *grade* is a term applied to standards of quality when more than one quality of a particular food is defined.

Cash versus Credit Buying

In a later chapter, we discuss installment buying. Buying on the installment plan may allow you to have what you want earlier than if you pay cash, but installment buying usually costs more than cash buying. If you can save and wait to pay cash, you can get more for your money.

Chapter Summary

Buying involves making many kinds of choices; it should be based on budgeting. Wisdom in buying involves determining your needs and going shopping to satisfy those needs rather than making impulse purchases. Some advertising messages are misleading, some are helpful and informative, and some are meaningless. Advertising should be studied carefully as a guide in buying. Some standards are measures of size, weight, and distance; others are measures of quality. Informative labels give information about standards, grades, content, and other characteristics of goods.

CHAPTER 5

THE VARIETIES OF INVESTMENTS

Up to this point, we have discussed the importance of saving and spending wisely. Once you have saved up some money, you must know what to do with it in order to create wealth. In this chapter, you will learn the various types of investments that you can make. The next chapter will focus on the ways in which decisions must be made in investing.

> **THERE CAN BE NO INVESTMENT WITHOUT SAVING**

Government Bonds

In addition to government savings bonds discussed in an earlier chapter, there are other types of government bonds that can be purchased as an investment. A bond represents a promise to pay the face value of the bond at some time in the future, with yearly interest at a specified rate. It has often been said that a government bond is as good as the government that issues it.

Generally, bonds issued by a federal government or central government rank at the top as to quality. However, there are many other good government bonds. Any broker or dealer selling bonds can provide information as to the reputation of the governmental unit in paying interest and in paying bonds when due.

Municipal Bonds Besides federal or central government bonds, there are bonds issued by other levels of government. Bonds issued by these other levels of government—states, cities, counties, etc. are referred to as municipal bonds or *muni's* for short.

Any government unit that issues a bond must make provisions to pay the interest and to pay the debt when it becomes due. The money for interest payments and debt retirement usually comes from taxation. The tax receipts of a governmental unit are comparable to the earnings of a business enterprise. The economic conditions within such a unit are comparable to the competitive conditions within an industry. Such factors have a definite effect upon the ability of the issuer of the bonds to pay interest and to repay the principal on the maturity date.

Because municipal bonds are usually considered safe investments, the rates of interest paid on these bonds are relatively low compared with corporation bonds which are generally more risky. However, the rates are often higher than can be earned on deposits in savings accounts.

Common Stock

Investment in common stock has certain complications that need not detain us here. Suffice it to say that when you buy stock in a corporation, you are actually buying a share in the ownership of the corporation. Common stock is issued in what are called shares. The extent of your ownership depends on the number of shares that you own in relation to the number of shares that have been issued and sold. For example, if 1,000 shares of common stock of a corporation have been issued and sold, and you own 100 shares, you own 10 percent interest in the corporation. A corporation makes no promise or guarantees that a dividend will be paid. Since a dividend is a share of profits, there may be none.

Preferred Stock

The varieties of preferred stock need not detain us here. We will simply focus of the main features of preferred stock. The owners of preferred stock have a share in the ownership of a corporation, but unlike the owners of common stock, they do not usually have a right to vote in the election of corporate directors. They do, however, have certain preferred claims, and that's how this stock gets its name. *Preferred* stock usually has a preference as to dividends; that is, the owners of preferred stock receive their stipulated and fixed share of the profits before the common stockholders are paid their dividends. Sometimes, the stock is preferred as to assets in case the corporation discontinues business. In other words, if the assets of the business are sold, the preferred stockholders will be paid before the common stockholders.

Closely Held and Publicly Held Corporations

A *closely held corporation* is one in which the stock is owned usually by a small group of people and sometimes by only one or two families. Those who own the greater share of the stock are generally the managers. Those who own the minority share of the stock have practically nothing to say with regard to the management, but take what dividends are allotted to them on the basis of their holdings. Those who operate the business may pay themselves large salaries and thus leave very little for dividends.

You should be aware of the fact that there is considerable risk in buying stock in a closely held corporation because of the difficulty in selling the stock if you should try to do so. There are not too many people who are eager to purchase stock in a corporation of this type since their stocks are not traded on organized stock exchanges, and the corporation need not publish financial statements.

The most common type of corporation is a publicly held corporation. A *publicly held corporation* or *public corporation* is one whose stock is available for public sale. The securities (bonds and stocks) of public corporations may be either listed on stock exchanges or unlisted; but even in the case of an unlisted security of a publicly held corporation, there is still a better market for these securities than for those of a closely held corporation.

Corporation Bonds

Bonds are evidence of a debt owed by the enterprise; they do not represent a share in the ownership of an enterprise. When a business issues bonds, it acknowledges that it owes the holders a certain sum of money and agrees to repay the sum on a certain date and under certain conditions. It also agrees to pay interest at a specified rate and at specified intervals.

Coupon Bonds An individual who owns a *coupon bond* can tear off each coupon as it becomes due and present it to his or her bank for the collection of interest.

Registered Bonds A *registered bond* is a bond that is recorded by the issuer in the name of the person to whom it has been sold. The interest on the bond will be paid only to the registered owner. From the point of view of theft, a registered bond is therefore safer than a coupon bond.

Mortgage Bonds When a bond is issued, the issuing corporation usually pledges some security, such as specific property or the right to certain earnings. A utility company may pledge some of its equipment or its real estate. When some property is pledged to the buyers of the bonds, these bonds are known as *mortgage bonds*.

Although certain property or rights are pledged to insure the safety of the principal of a mortgage bond, various problems arise if the bondholders are forced to take over the property or the rights in case the interest is not paid.

Debenture Bonds Some bonds are issued by corporations without any specific pledge of property. The bonds are backed by the general credit, reputation, and assets of the corporation. Bonds of this type are called *debenture bonds*.

Note: There are other types of bonds, but the list presented above gives a good picture of various types of corporation bonds that you can buy.

Bond Purchase Considerations

We have listed some types of corporate bonds that you can purchase. Here are some important factors to consider when buying corporation bonds:

1. Record of past earnings of the company and the likelihood of future earnings.
2. Record of past market prices of the bonds.
3. Competitive and general business conditions.
4. Marketability of the bonds.
5. Credit rating of the issuing corporation.

Priority Claims on Earnings In most jurisdictions, dividends cannot be paid on either preferred stock or common stock unless all interest has been paid on outstanding bonds. It is also a general rule that dividends cannot be paid on common stock unless those on preferred stock have been paid.

In other words, bondholders have first claim on earnings, before preferred stockholders; preferred stockholders have second claim on earnings, before common stockholders; and common stockholders receive dividends only to the extent that there are sufficient earnings to pay them. Dividends are never promised nor guaranteed. In years of low profitability, the preferred stockholders are therefore more likely than common stockholders to get their dividends: In years of high profitability, however, common stockholders have the possibility of getting much more than what is paid to preferred stockholders.

Mutual Funds

One of the principles of investment is not to place all your eggs in one basket. This is a call for diversification in investment holdings. It is good advice but many small investors are not able to buy a variety of stocks or bonds. Therefore, these investors may prefer to buy shares of stock in investment companies or mutual funds. The money received from the sale of shares in an investment company or a mutual fund is invested in a great variety of securities. The owner of a share in one of these companies is a part owner of a company that owns several different types of securities. These companies are called *investment companies* or *mutual funds*. They vary widely as to their method or organization, their management, the type of securities they buy, and the methods by which ownership shares are sold. In all cases, however, the purpose is to obtain money from investors, which is then reinvested in a variety of securities so that the investor in the investment fund owns a share in a wide list of securities.

The purpose of an investment company is therefore to provide a wide diversification of investment that is managed by experts, so that an individual who has only a small investment to make and who is not an expert may have these advantages. However, in selecting an investment company in which to invest funds, it is desirable to study the purposes and organization by consulting a reliable broker. Each mutual fund follows certain policies. One investment company may invest its funds principally in conservative securities that do not pay especially high dividends, but another may invest its funds in speculative securities that may have greater opportunity for growth in value.

Small Business Investing

For some people, owning and operating a small business is one of the most important dreams and objectives in their lives. These people may be able to save their money until they have enough to go into business for themselves. Before anyone decides to invest his or her life savings by buying or starting a business, however, he or she should make a very careful study of all the problems involved. To own and operate a small business is not easy, and one should have some experience in the business before attempting to operate it alone.

People with money are frequently tempted to buy an interest in a partnership, or stock in a small corporation in which a friend is interested, or to lend money to a friend or a relative in business. Such investments should be made with the utmost care.

Investing in a partnership often involves complicated legal responsibilities. Even though one of the partners may not be actively engaged in the business, under the laws of many jurisdictions, he or she is equally responsible with the other partners for debts of the firm. For instance, suppose that you become a part owner of a business and allow your partner to operate it. The business fails to make a profit, and the creditors demand payment. If your partner cannot pay, the creditors can demand payment from you.

Many people with experience will advocate not investing in the enterprise of a friend or relative. The friend or the relative usually feels that he or she has the right to operate the business as he or she sees fit. He or she may legally have the right, but sooner or later, trouble may arise.

Real Estate

Many people save their money to be able to invest in real estate. If you are planning the purchase of real estate as an investment, you should consider the following seven points, after both the desirability of the location and the quality of the property, have been determined.

1. Can the property be rented?
2. At what price can the property be rented?
3. What will be the annual cost of repairs?
4. What will be the taxes?
5. What will be the annual loss from depreciation?
6. Approximately what percent of the time will the property be vacant?
7. What will be the approximate net earnings?

Real estate prices tend to fluctuate. Therefore, the current cost of a piece of property is no indication of its future value. The community may change rapidly with a resulting decrease or increase in the value of the property. Because of a change in business conditions, the value of the property may be raised or lowered.

The purchase of unimproved real estate (with no buildings) is usually a speculative investment made in the hope that it can be resold at a profit. A person well acquainted with managing property may find real estate more suitable than any other type of investment; but if one is not in a position to manage real estate with buildings on it, it may not prove to be a desirable investment.

Mortgage Notes and Bonds

A *mortgage note* is a written promise to pay with interest the specified sum that is secured by the specific property described in the mortgage. A mortgage makes it impossible for one to sell property on which the mortgage is given without payment of the loan that it secures. *Mortgage bonds* may be used instead of notes.

When people borrow money on real estate, they usually sign (a) a mortgage and (b) a note or series of notes. They give both the mortgage and the note or notes to the ones from whom they are borrowing the money. The *mortgage* is a written contract giving the lender permission to acquire ownership of or to dispose of the property to satisfy the debt in case the debt is not paid as agreed.

There are first-mortgage notes, second-mortgage notes, and third-mortgage notes. The first mortgage note is the most common. The loan that it represents should not normally exceed 80 or 90 percent of the appraised value of the property.

A first mortgage has the first claim against the assets. The holder of the second mortgage cannot be paid until the claim of the first mortgage is settled. Interest rates are lower on first mortgages because those mortgages have first claims.

Mortgage bonds are usually issued be a mortgage company that lends the money to the mortgagee and who in turn sells mortgage bonds to investors. The value of mortgage bonds is measured by the value of the property behind them and the ability of this property to provide funds for the payment of the interest and the principal on the due dates.

Chapter Summary

There is a wide variety of investment vehicles through which you can acquire and preserve wealth. The purchase of government bonds allows you to earn interest, and they are relatively safe. Common and preferred stocks are other investment vehicles. Holders of preferred stocks are paid before holders of common stock. In addition to stocks, corporation bonds are a common investment vehicle. Stocks imply ownership whereas bonds do not. Other investment vehicles are mutual funds or investment companies, small businesses, real estate, and mortgage notes and bonds.

CHAPTER 6

THE INVESTMENT DECISION

In the previous chapter, we looked at the kinds and choices of investments. In this chapter, we focus on the investment decision and investment procedure. Stated differently, the previous chapter answers the *what* of investment whereas this chapter addresses the *how* of investment.

> **THE HIGHER THE RISK, THE GREATER THE RETURN**

Investing versus Speculating

There is a difference between investing and speculating and you should be aware of that difference. *Investing* is buying assets such as securities with the expectation of receiving a certain, though maybe small, income over a long period. *Speculating* is buying securities or other assets with the hope that the value of those securities or assets will increase in a relatively short period. In both cases, there are risks, but the risks increase as the possibilities of large gains or losses increase.

When we speak of investing, we ordinarily think of securities although there are many investments in real estate and other property as we saw in the previous chapter. It is rather difficult to define securities. We have already used the term security in another sense as being the property pledged to a lender. For purposes of investments, however, we use the term security in a slightly different way. A *security*, for investment purposes, refers to stocks, bonds, notes, and mortgages, which indicate either ownership or indebtedness. These examples of securities represent some kind of pledge, promise, agreement, or right. They can be bought and sold if they have any value. Many financial advisers would not recommend a person making investments in securities until an adequate amount of insurance had been purchased and a savings program set up to cover financial emergencies. The importance of a savings program in wealth creation is again evident.

Income, Safety, and Growth

We must assume that investors, on average, will not gamble, but that they will be interested in the income and safety of their investment. They may also be interested in a security that will grow in value. If investors were interested in the safest investment at a low income, they would probably buy high-grade bonds. If they were interested in investments that will probably increase in value (with some risk), they would probably buy good stocks or invest in good real estate. Because of the peculiarities of people buying on the stock market, there are some stocks that pay a good rate of dividend based on the price of the stock. These are excellent stocks, but buyers do not expect them to increase in value to any great extent in the future. Therefore, they are not popular with many buyers who want stocks that they think will increase in value.

Generally, government bonds of various types are considered among the most conservative investments. Therefore, let us look at corporation securities in order to determine their merits in regard to growth, income, and safety. Their relative merits are indicated in a general way in Table 6.1.

Table 6.1
Merits of Corporation Securities

SECURITY	GROWTH	INCOME	SAFETY
Preferred Stock	Steady	Steady	Good
Common Stock	Best	Variable	Least
Bonds	Usually none	Very steady	Best

Sources of Information for Investment

In order to make good decisions about investing, you require good information. There are two main sources of professional help to which you can turn without obligation. One is an investment broker and the other is a bank. The broker and the bank receive their compensation as a commission on any purchase or sale of securities.

An *investment broker* is a person or firm specializing in the study of securities, advising investors, and arranging for the purchase or the sale of securities. A stockbroker provides some of the same services as an investment broker. In fact, a stockbroker and an investment broker are often the same.

There are specialists in some banks who devote their time to serving as investment advisers. The selection of a broker or a bank may be difficult for a new investor. The best procedure is probably to talk with friends and get their advice based on their past experience.

The price of a share of stock does not necessarily indicate whether it is a good or bad investment. For example, two equally good corporations of exactly the same size may have common stocks that are selling for widely different prices. A share of a stock of one corporation might be selling for $20 a share with two million shares outstanding. One share of stock of the other corporation may be selling at $40 a share with one million shares of stock outstanding.

If one prefers to do so, he or she can make a study of his or her own in regard to various kinds of securities. For the average investor, this is too great a task because there are many thousands of kinds of stocks, bonds, and other securities for sale. However, there are excellent monthly financial services available to which one can subscribe to obtain current investment information. There is also good financial information available in some newspapers. Most city libraries have financial information regarding earnings, dividends paid, stock outstanding, assets, and credit ratings of corporations. If you are going to do your own studying and investing, you will need to confine your attention to a few securities in order to make a thorough analysis.

If you are in doubt about whether a security is legally offered for sale or whether the person promoting its sale is using honest and legal methods, it is possible to investigate the sale of the stock by contacting the U. S. Securities and Exchange Commission (SEC), the state securities commission, The Canadian Securities Administrators (CSA), the provincial securities regulators (in Canada), the local Better Business Bureau, a reliable broker, a banker, or the local stock exchange.

Safety of Principal

The safety of the principal invested in a bond of a corporation, whether it is a mortgage bond or a debenture bond, is really only as good as the corporation itself. The same can be said of common and preferred stocks. We have already learned that common stock may increase or decrease in value in dollar terms. The face value of bonds, however, will not increase in value in terms of dollars. Preferred stocks have preferred claims on earnings or assets or both, but they may decrease in value if the corporation has financial trouble.

The safety of the principal is also involved in any other kind of investment. For example, a person's investment in a government bond is only as safe as the government itself. Cities, counties, states, and provinces have credit and financial ratings just the same as businesses.

There are three main factors to be considered as to the safety of the principal when one invests in real estate. First is the question as to whether the investor receives a good legal title to the property; second is the question of location; and third is the question of economic conditions. Checking on the title often entails legal assistance, and in checking on the location one should make sure that it is in a location that will not decrease in value. For instance, some residential neighborhoods are gradually depreciating in value while others are increasing in value principally because of the location. Economic conditions affect the value of real estate just as they affect the value of all other investments.

The Dollar-Averaging Principle

When stocks are purchased as an investment (as opposed to the speculator or trader who buys and sells with the idea of making a profit by buying and selling), they are usually held for a long period of time. Prices of stock may change considerably. The buyer may, for example, pay $85 a share for stock and may want to keep it because he thinks it is good. The price may go up or down. For example, it may go down to $80 a share, at which time he may buy more stock. If he owns 100 shares at $85 and buys 100 shares at $80, his average cost is $82.50 a share. This process is called *dollar averaging*.

It must be remembered that there is a broker's fee for buying stocks. In the short run (months as opposed to years) the dollar-averaging principle may not work to a small investor's advantage because of the high brokerage fee on small purchases.

Income from Investment

You must keep in mind that the safety of the principal is more important than a satisfactory income. The fact is, if the principal is lost, there will be no income.

Rate of Return A sound investment does not have a yield that is higher than the average rate of interest used to attract investors. A conservative rate of interest on a good bond will be determined by the conditions that exist at the time the bond is offered for sale. A high-grade bond sometimes pays no more than 4 or 5 percent interest on the face value, but these rates are variable. Remember, however, that even though the stated interest on a bond may be only 5 percent, the bond may be sold at a discount so that the rate of return on the investment is actually higher than the stated amount. On the other hand, if one has to pay a premium for the bond, the rate of return on the investment will be lower than the stated amount. When the rate of return offered on a bond is much above the rate of interest on high-grade government bonds, special care should be taken in investigating the quality of the security.

Regularity of Income A corporation makes no promise as to the amount of dividends, if any, that will be paid on common stock. There will not be any dividends paid unless there are sufficient earnings from which to pay them. Bondholders must receive their interest first, and the preferred stockholders must be paid their dividends before common stockholders receive anything.

Most investors are interested in having a steady and reliable income. The continuous payment of interest or dividends is therefore one of the first considerations in evaluating a security.

The past history of a corporation in earnings and dividends can be determined from the records of any stock listed on an exchange, but expert advice is needed to determine the possible future earnings.

Margin of Safety For investment purposes, a good corporation should earn considerably more money than is paid out as bond interest and stock dividends. Unless the corporation is regularly earning more than is needed for these purposes, there is not an adequate margin of safety.

Marketability of Securities

An investor, in the true sense of the word, is not interested in buying a security with the thought of selling it immediately. However, you must consider this possibility.

For most investors, the most desirable securities are those that are listed for public sale on stock exchanges or at least those securities that are sold directly through brokers. The least desirable securities for the small investor would be the stock in a closely held corporation unless he or she is closely associated with that particular business. Real estate would be a poor investment for a person who might suddenly need the money and then find it difficult to sell the real estate at a satisfactory price.

Buying and Selling Securities

Stock Exchanges Two main types of securities exist in the United States through which stocks and bonds are easily bought and sold. They are the local stock exchanges in various cities and the national exchanges located in New York City. The Canadian Stock Exchange consists of mainly four stock exchanges, the largest of which is the Toronto Stock Exchange (TSX). Stock exchanges exist in other countries as well.

Buying and selling stocks on a security exchange is carried on by means of the *auction method*. A stock may be offered for sale at a certain price, or someone may bid for the same stock at a different price. A sale is made when someone buys the stock at the price offered. These offers and bids are going on regularly so that anyone owning a stock has a pretty good idea of the price at which the stock can be sold.

Brokers deal on stock exchanges. They represent buyers and sellers of securities. Banks will also handle these transactions through a broker. In order for brokers to deal on an exchange, they must be members of the exchange. If they are not members, they can deal through other brokers who are members.

Chapter Conclusion

Knowledge of investments is important in wealth acquisition. Government bonds are a conservative type of investment. Stocks, bonds, and mortgage notes represent the various securities of a corporation available for investment purposes. Speculative securities are primarily for people who can afford to take a chance on the growth in value of securities. Most people seeking to acquire wealth should invest, but should not speculate or gamble.

CHAPTER 7

CREDIT FUNDAMENTALS

In our post-modern world, the use of credit is widespread. Different forms of credit exist, and you can use credit as a means of achieving your financial objectives. In order for credit to work in your favour, you must understand certain aspects of credit. This chapter is designed to provide you with the fundamentals of credit.

> **THE USE OF CREDIT ESTABLISHES A DEBT**

Importance of Credit

There can be little doubt that credit is a vital force in our economy. It is of economic and social importance to every family and business organization. The first use of credit in business transactions was to increase the flexibility of barter (the exchange of goods for goods). The use of credit preceded the use of money. The custom of charging interest began early, and the cost of credit is something that has been reckoned with in all of recorded history.

Credit is either an advance (loan) of money with which to purchase goods and services or an advance of goods and services in exchange for a promise to pay at a later date. The use of credit by consumers is similar to its use by governments and by private business organizations. Whenever an immediate need for cash, goods, or services is met through the proper use of credit, the economy of the nation is strengthened and the level of living is raised. The immediate need is actually met because of the faith one person has in the honesty and responsibility of another—faith that the debt will be repaid at maturity or that each installment payment on the debt will be paid as it becomes due.

Credit first became important when people developed need for cash to help them meet financial emergencies for which they were unprepared. More recently, its importance has increased as people have used the installment plan as a means of adjusting the high and low points that develop in their spending patterns. This is illustrated in the purchase of an automobile at a relatively high price that is paid over a period of many months in relatively small payments. Similarly, the installment plan is used in the purchase of insurance when an individual pays monthly, semi-annual, or annual premiums throughout a lifetime so that he or she may have a large amount of protection from the very beginning of the life of his or her policy.

Insurance premiums are based on the past experience of large groups who have shared risks. Thus, it is possible to determine accurately the amount of the installment payments or premiums that an individual must pay to maintain his or her financial protection. It has become a matter of concern whenever consumer resistance to the use of credit tends to slow down the purchasing of automobiles, homes, and other major items.

Forms of Credit

The term "credit" is often used to refer to one's ability to borrow money or to buy goods on time. In other words, it means credit standing or the ability to use credit. A debt is incurred whenever an individual makes use of his or her credit standing. Each exchange of economic goods or services that is based on credit remains incomplete until such time as full payment of the debt is made. Many consumers buy on credit because it is more convenient to pay for several purchases at one time at some future date than it is to pay for each purchase separately. Consumers also frequently buy on credit because it is a convenient way to buy or because they do not have cash available to pay for a purchase immediately. In either case, a debt is incurred. Consumers often borrow cash with which to pay current bills, to buy goods and services, to meet emergencies, or to consolidate existing debts.

Classification of Credit

In general, *consumer credit* is debt that is incurred by a consumer for a home, goods, or services for personal and family use and consumption. For certain purposes, however, consumer credit is considered to comprise debts for goods and services for personal and family use having a maturity of less than five years. Such debts may be classified as *short-term credit* and *intermediate-term credit*. A debt on an owner-occupied home that is financed by a long-term loan secured by a real estate mortgage is not always considered to be consumer credit. Debt incurred for repair or modernization of an owner-occupied home ordinarily matures within a few months and, therefore, is generally classified as consumer credit.

The extensive credit needs of salary and wage earners are met through the use of numerous forms of credit. Involved with consumers in using the different forms of credit are retail merchants, commercial banks, consumer finance companies, sales finance companies, credit unions, pawnbrokers, and others. With its many aspects and in its many forms, credit is truly one of the important tools of money management used by consumers.

Installment Debt

Debts on which payments are to be made at periodic intervals are known as *installment debts* or *installment credit*. Such consumer debts may arise from purchases of goods and services for personal and family consumption or from obtaining loans for the payment of such purchases. The arrangement for repaying this kind of debt ordinarily includes finance charges, stipulated regular payments, and the use of some form of contract that provides for legal action where there is default in payment.

Much installment credit involves arrangements between consumers and retail merchants for purchases of automobiles and other consumer goods. An even larger portion of the volume of installment credit consists of cash loans from commercial banks, credit unions, sales finance companies, and consumer finance companies. The money borrowed is used to buy goods, to meet emergencies, and to consolidate debts.

Non-installment Debt

Debts for which the full payment is to be made in a single payment at a specified maturity date are known as *non-installment debts* or *non-installment credit*. A cash loan to be repaid in a single payment may be made to a consumer by a commercial bank, pawnbroker, savings and loan association, or miscellaneous lender for any one of many good reasons. Also, non-installment credit is used by consumers whenever they arrange to make a single payment for goods that are charged at a retail store; for gas, electricity, telephone or internet service; or for a hospital, medical, or other similar debt.

The Charge Account

Many retail outlets and business enterprises sell merchandise on *open account* or on *charge account*. This means that at the time of the sale, the title to the merchandise passes to the purchaser, and the store accepts the customer's promise to pay for it later, usually 30 days. The customer is required to sign the sales slip as evidence that he or she received the merchandise.

A *service account* is similar to a charge account except that the charges made to it are for services rendered, such as legal, medical, or accounting services.

The privilege of charging purchases may be withdrawn by a business enterprise at any time the customer fails to pay the amount he or she owes in accordance with the terms of the account. A brief summary of the advantages of a charge account to a customer follows.

1. A charge account is a very convenient and simple way to buy.
2. A record of purchases is made automatically.
3. Payment for purchases may be delayed until a future specified time.
4. Charge accounts make it easier to order merchandise by mail or telephone or the Internet.
5. Money is not needed at the time of purchase; therefore the danger of loss while shopping is minimized.
6. Salespeople and store owners learning to know charge account customers may result in improved service.
7. Payment for several purchases may be made at one time.
8. The privilege of charging purchases may add to one's prestige.

A charge account may be a disadvantage for a person who has a tendency to spend without regard to his or her income or ability to pay.

Types of Charge Accounts

Different types of charge accounts exist. In this section, we review revolving charge accounts, budget charge accounts, divided charge accounts, and credit-bank plans. Let us begin with the revolving charge account.

Revolving Charge Account

The revolving charge account is in use in some places. Under this plan, payment for purchases may be extended to four, five, or even six months. The consumer and the store representative determine at the time the account is opened the maximum amount that may be owed to the store at any one time. To illustrate the revolving charge account, let us assume that the maximum amount that may be owed is set at $240 and that the store will allow the consumer a maximum of six months to pay for purchases. Equal monthly payments of $40 (240 ÷ 6 months) are to be made whenever there is an unpaid balance in the account at the end of a month. New purchases to be charged to the account may be made at any time provided that the total amount owed by the customer does not exceed the established maximum of $240. Usually, a service charge of some kind is charged each month for this type of account.

Budget Charge Account

A *budget charge account* is a system of credit under which regular purchases can be made. Payments must be made in monthly installments based on the size of the account balance. Interest is charged on the monthly balance.

Divided Charge Account

One charge account plan permits a consumer to charge a large item like a refrigerator or a living room suite and then pay one third of the cost in each of the succeeding three months. This plan is known as a *divided charge account*. Usually no service charge is added for the final two months.

Credit-Bank Plan

A *credit-bank plan* is a type of charge account in which the bank pays the customer's bills when they are submitted to it. This charge account service is available only in those retail stores that agree to participate in the credit-bank plan.

Credit Terms

No down payment is required for purchases through a charge or open account. The time allowed between the date of purchase on a charge account and the date the payment is due is the length of the *credit term*. The usual credit term for charge accounts is 30 days; however, it may be for a different period of time. A charge account ordinarily carries no service charge. The customer is expected to pay the full amount he or she has charged at the end of each credit term. In many stores, if this part of the bargain is not fulfilled, a service charge is made on the past-due balance and added on at the next billing.

Under a plan known as *cycle billing*, the balance owed by a certain customer falls due regularly on a certain day of the month regardless of the date of the last purchase. This means that a bill for a purchase made late in a customer's credit month becomes due in much less than 30 days. The reason some stores use cycle billing on charge accounts is to spread the work of preparing monthly statements over the entire month for the accounting department.

Credit Cards

Perhaps the first thing that comes to mind when you hear of a credit card is Visa or MasterCard, or American Express. But many other credit cards exist. A *credit card* is issued by some business firms, such as banks, oil companies, restaurants, hotels, airlines, etc. The card identifies customers particularly when they are travelling, thus enabling them to charge purchases of goods and services even though they are not known in the city where the purchase is made. There is no charge for most of these credit cards. The credit card companies bill their customers monthly, and the customers are expected to pay the entire amount upon receipt of the statement or within 25 days of the billing date. If for some reason the full amount cannot be paid, the company will add on a service charge to be paid along with the unpaid balance at the next monthly billing date.

Other organizations such as Visa, MasterCard, and American Express issue the more general-use type of credit card. These cards allow cardholders to charge meals, hotel rooms, airline tickets, groceries, car rentals and a host of other things. The bills are sent to the credit card company, which sends a monthly bill for all purchases to the person holding the credit card. The card-holding consumer usually pays a relatively small annual fee.

Cost of Charge Accounts

Selling on credit adds extra costs to every sale. The following are the main reasons for extra costs:

a) The clerical work necessary for recording sales and collecting accounts
b) Loss of interest on the money that is invested in accounts receivable from customers
c) Losses due to bad debts

d) The greater tendency of charge customers to return goods for exchange.

Some stores set their sales prices high enough to cover the cost of charge accounts; others use a two-price system, one for cash sales and the other for sales on account. Let us assume that an item is priced at $159.95 cash or $164.95 if charged, payable in 30 days. The actual cost of charging the purchase to the customer's account is $5. This really means that he or she is paying $5 for the use of $159.95 for 30 days. This works out to an annual rate of interest of 37.5 percent.

In stores that do not carefully investigate customers' ability to pay before charging sales to their accounts, the losses from failure to collect debts are likely to be great. One may well expect to find high prices in stores that recklessly advertise generous credit terms to everyone. Stores that have sound credit policies have practically no losses from bad debts. We need not assume, therefore, that a merchant who sells on credit must necessarily sell at higher prices than a merchant who sells for cash.

If selling on credit increases sales, the total overhead cost of each sale may actually be decreased. The costs of selling on credit, however, are reported by some stores to be as much as 6% to 8% higher than costs of selling for cash. On the other hand, stores that regularly sell on credit often provide delivery services and other conveniences. These services, combined with possible higher costs because of charge accounts, may cause the store to sell at higher prices than a cash-and-carry store.

Chapter Summary

Credit plays an important role in helping you on the road to wealth acquisition. Through credit, you can obtain goods and services now to be paid for at a later date. Credit enables you to acquire assets that can improve your standard of living now and in the future. There are many different forms of credit but not all types may be suitable for you. Credit cards, if used wisely, can prove to be a very useful ally en route to acquiring and preserving wealth.

CHAPTER 8

THE WISE USE OF CREDIT

Credit can be good or bad depending on how you use it. The wise use of credit can facilitate the wealth-creation process. On the other hand, poor use of credit can literally ruin an individual. It is of utmost importance to know how to use credit wisely. This chapter will provide some important insights on the wise use of credit.

> **CREDIT CAN FACILITATE WEALTH CREATION**

Your Credit Standing

Our *credit standing* or *creditworthiness* is an indication of our ability to secure goods, services, and money in return for a promise to pay. It represents our ability to incur debts because some lender trusts us. A favorable credit standing does not come automatically. It comes as the result of slow growth. It must be nurtured, fostered, strengthened, and improved. It is an asset of tremendous value to those who develop it over a long period of years. It can be destroyed easily; it is sensitive to abuse; and it usually continues only as long as it is justified. A favorable credit standing over a period of time is enjoyed only by those who deserve it and who protect it.

A commonly recognized formula for determining the creditworthiness of an individual or a business enterprise consists of the "three Cs"—**c**haracter, **c**apacity, and **c**apital. Let us discuss each in turn, beginning with character.

Character

Character is revealed in one's conduct, attitudes, and achievements. It does not necessarily have any relation to one's wealth. It represents the sum total of the principles for which one stands. Your reputation is the result of how other people evaluate your character traits. You would not be able to borrow money or buy goods and services with the promise to pay later if others judge your character to be questionable. The importance of one's character is summed up in the Biblical passage:

> *A good name is rather to be chosen than great riches,*
> *and loving favour than silver and gold. (Proverbs 22:1)*

Capacity

Capacity is merely another term for earning power. It expresses your ability to earn and pay obligations when they become due. You may have an honorable character and perfectly good intentions of paying an obligation; but unless you have the ability or capacity to pay, you will not be able to pay satisfactorily. It is often more difficult to judge character objectively than it is to judge capacity. Capacity, or earning power, can be measured reasonably accurately (by income or wealth, for example), but character is an intangible quality.

Capital

The third measuring standard, *capital*, applies only to people who have property. Naturally, your net worth or capital affects your ability to pay debts when they become due and, consequently, affects your credit standing. People with a temporary lack of earning power but having a substantial net worth may still have a favorable credit standing; that is, others will still be willing to make loans to them or to sell to them based on their promise to pay.

Capacity and capital without character will affect your credit standing adversely, making it difficult to borrow money or buy goods and services on time.

Your Line of Credit

Your credit standing or creditworthiness refers to the chances or the probability that you will pay a debt when it becomes due. We have just learned that it depends upon the trust or confidence others have in your intention to pay. *Line of credit* means the maximum amount a lender or creditor will permit a customer to owe him or her at any one time.

Every responsible family should establish its line of credit with a good retail store or retail credit association regardless of whether it is used extensively or not. By so doing you will also take your first step in establishing your line of credit with a bank.

To establish your credit standing and your line of credit, the usual procedure is to go to your favorite store and discuss the matter frankly with the credit manager or the owner, who will request information of a personal nature about your character, capacity, and capital. Such information should be provided accurately and completely. The credit manager must have such information as a basis for determining how much credit to extend to you.

Credit Rating Agencies

There are agencies that provide credit rating information on businesses and also on individuals. Banks sometimes give confidential information on individuals and businesses. It is therefore important to maintain satisfactory relations with your bank if you desire a good credit rating.

Private credit agencies collect information and issue confidential reports for the benefit of their subscribers. Each subscriber contributes information about customers to the agency. Additional information is gathered from local newspapers, notices of change of address, death notices, and court record. Such information is valuable to retailers in protecting themselves from loss on accounts. If their customers move, they will want to know of the change in address. If customers die, the retailers would want to be sure that their claims are presented. If a person is taking court action against one of his or her customers, that person will want to protect his or her own claim.

The Associated Credit Bureaus of America (ACB) has more than 4,000 credit bureau members serving hundreds of thousands of business firms. Any of these local credit bureaus can develop a report on any individual in North America and in many foreign countries within a short period of time. Through the interchange of information, the credit records of millions of consumers are already compiled and are readily available to all members of the Associated Credit Bureaus of America. The services of this nationwide credit reporting system are an advantage to you if you have safeguarded your credit. You can move from one community to another, and your credit record will follow you or it can be checked upon very easily. However, a bad credit reputation also will follow you wherever you go.

Responsibility for Debts

It has long been recognized that individuals are morally and ethically responsible for the payment of their debts. The enactment of laws also reinforces one's legal responsibility for debts. In many jurisdictions, it is still the case that a husband is responsible for debts incurred by his wife unless he gives legal written notice that from the date of the notice forward he will not be responsible for them. A merchant, therefore, may sell on account to a man's wife with confidence that the husband is responsible for payment.

Parents generally are legally responsible for debts incurred by their children when permission has been given to the children to make purchases and to charge them to the parent's account. For instance, if it has been customary for a child to use a charge account of the parents, the parents are responsible for the debts. But there are exceptions to this general rule as indicated below.

Children are often referred to as minors. A *minor* is a person who is not yet old enough to be considered an adult under the laws of the society in which he or she lives. Stated differently, a minor is someone who has not yet reached the age of majority. Parents are generally responsible for debts incurred by minors.

Garnishment

If a debtor refuses to pay his or her debt, the creditor may succeed in having a court order issued requiring the employer of the debtor to pay part of the debtor's wages to the creditor until the debt has been paid. This procedure is called *garnishment* or *garnisheeing* of wages. In most cases, there are guidelines governing the amount that can be garnished.

Attachment

If you own property and you owe a debt and refuse to pay or cannot pay as agreed, you may be sued in court to force you to pay it. A common procedure in such a case is to ask the court for an attachment on some of your property until the case is settled. Simply stated, an *attachment* is a legal process whereby the property attached comes under the control of the court until the case is settled. Property upon which an attachment order has been placed may not be sold and may not be moved except by court approval. The court can order the property sold to pay the debt.

Statutes of Limitations

The statutes of limitations set a time limit after which a creditor cannot enforce a legal claim. For example, in some jurisdictions, if an account is not settled within five years, the creditor cannot sue for the amount. If the debtor, however, makes a payment or a promise to pay during the five-year period or at any time thereafter, the account is revived or reinstated.

Bankruptcy

People are *insolvent* if they are unable to pay their debts when they become due. If their debts are greater than the total fair value of their assets, a court may declare them to be *bankrupt*. Recognizing the impossibility of paying his debts, a man may ask the court to declare him bankrupt. This process is known as *voluntary bankruptcy*. If you owe a creditor on a past due account, it is possible for the creditor to ask the court to declare you bankrupt. This process is known as *involuntary bankruptcy*.

Bankruptcy discharges all of a debtor's former debts and enables him or her to start to acquire property again. But you should not look upon bankruptcy as an easy way out of paying your debt obligations. When bankruptcy has been filed against a person, he or she will have to operate on a cash basis for a number of years. This can be quite inconvenient since it means that in most cases, he or she would be denied the use of charge accounts, credit cards, loans for automobiles, homes, and other consumer goods.

Problems with Credit

The use of credit tends to increase purchases and to stimulate business. If consumer debt increases too fast and is not being paid off, this situation indicates that buyers on credit are not able to pay their debts. Such a condition would, therefore, be an indication that we might be entering a period of bad business conditions.

The wise thing to do is to keep purchases and payments in balance. When individuals cannot pay their debts, the businesses that sold to them may suffer a loss. Therefore, when great numbers of people buy more on credit than they can repay, we experience an overexpansion of consumer credit. The result may be that many businesses lose money because they cannot collect for goods sold on credit. We are all affected adversely by bad business conditions that arise when great numbers of people cannot pay their debts.

Chapter Summary

Consumer credit is debt that is incurred for a home, goods, or services for personal and family use and consumption. In its many forms, credit is a useful tool if one stays in command of it, does not use it unnecessarily, and gets it at low cost. Because it is convenient and often is a means of adjusting high and low points in spending, credit is used by people in all income categories. Each credit transaction remains incomplete until such time as all legal responsibilities and repayment obligations of the debt are fulfilled. A good credit rating must be earned and maintained if one wants to obtain credit when it is needed and to get it at a reasonable cost. If it becomes impossible for an individual to pay his or her debts, prompt action should be taken to notify creditors and to establish an adjusted payment schedule that can be met.

When credit is used as a substitute for good money management, there is usually a tendency to make excessive use of it. When overextension of credit forces a person to declare bankruptcy, there is a weakening of the economic and social structure.

CHAPTER 9

ELEMENTS OF INSTALLMENT CREDIT

In our modern society, many people buy now and then make arrangements to pay on a regular basis over a period of time. They may borrow money to finance certain expenditures and make arrangements to repay the loan by regular payments over a certain time period. These

> **AN INSTALLMENT PLAN MAY BE HELPFUL**

arrangements are the essence of installment credit. In this chapter, we will discuss how installment credit can be used advantageously to create wealth, and how it may result in serious trouble. Let us begin by examining the nature of installment buying.

The Nature of Installment Buying

There are fundamental differences between buying on an installment plan and buying on charge account. The following facts about buying on an installment plan are significant:

1. A down payment is usually required
2. A finance or carrying charge is added to the price
3. Payments of equal amounts are spread over a period of time
4. Security for the amount of the unpaid balance is taken by the seller in the form of a security agreement.

The Importance of Installment Buying

Buying on an installment plan has become popular and is the norm for many purchases. Most transactions today are credit transactions, and most of these credit transactions are in the form of installment credit. Large ticket items such as automobiles, furniture, and many household appliances are usually purchased on the installment plan.

Some Problems of Installment Buying

Mass production enables us to get the goods and services we want at a price we can afford to pay. But mass production is not possible except when people can buy freely. Many families cannot pay cash for major items such as automobiles, furniture, and appliances. Under the installment plan, however, these families are able to purchase without cash. The opportunity for consumers to buy now and to pay later has increased mass consumption of goods and services. If credit privileges and installment plans of purchasing were to be withdrawn and purchases were to be made entirely on a cash basis, sales would decrease rapidly, and business activity would slow down. Thus we see that consumer credit, mass production, and mass distribution are closely related.

Some experts believe that selling goods and services to consumers on an installment plan is one of the major factors in making our high standard of living possible. They argue that installment selling increases the consumption of goods, which in turn increases production and thus tends to lower costs, and that the greater production is, the more jobs there are at good wage rates.

There are some people who argue that many families would never save enough to make major purchases, but when they purchase on an installment plan, they are obliged to pay the installments when they come due.

Of course, government officials, bankers, and business people express concern about excessive purchasing on the installment plan. They reason that if the incomes of many people who owe money on installment contracts would be reduced or if they lost their jobs, these people would probably not be able to make their payments. If great numbers of people are not able to pay their installment debts, there is a possibility that businesses cannot collect their debts and will therefore lose money. If businesses lose enough money or fail to make a satisfactory profit, the possibility of the economy falling into a recession is increased.

Installment Contracts

An installment contract sets forth the specific terms of the purchase, including the following:

- Amount of the down payment
- Dates of future payments
- Amounts of future payments
- Finance charges
- Protection to the seller in case payments are not made as scheduled.

The seller is protected by a security agreement. A *security agreement* is a written statement signed by the buyer indicating that the seller has rights to repossession as well as rights to sue for the purchase price. This signed agreement must also include a general description of the article being sold. Thus, most installment sales are called *secured credit sales* because of this written, signed security agreement. In a secured credit sale the possession and risk of loss pass to the buyer, but the seller has a security interest in the article until he or she has been paid in full.

Features of Installment Contracts

Installment contracts are usually written in triplicate. One copy is kept by the purchaser; another copy is filed in some local recording office; and the third copy is kept by the seller. The purpose of recording an installment contract is to make the record public so that anyone can determine whether a claim has been made against the property listed as security.

Installment contracts differ as to their wording and content, but a similarity is found in all types. In each case, the purchaser must agree to do certain things. For example, he or she must agree to make the payments as specified; the balance of the contract may be due if one payment is missed; there may be a claim against the salary or wages of the purchaser if payments are not made; and the purchaser has to keep taxes paid and the property insured for damage or loss and free from other claims.

Questions to Ask Before Signing an Installment Contract

1. What is the cash price of the item?
2. How much money is actually advanced?
3. What are the total finance or carrying charges?
4. What are the other charges such as insurance, legal, and recording charges in addition to the purchase price and carrying charges?
5. How do the installment costs compare with costs on other plans such as a personal loan at a bank?
6. Are all the facts about the contract known and fully understood?

7. Are all figures in the contract correct? Are all blank spaces filled in?
8. Specifically what security has been given?
9. May wages be assigned in case of delinquent payments?
10. Does the buyer have the option of paying the total amount due and settling the contract at a reduction in cost?
11. Will a fair notice be given before repossession?
12. What rights does the buyer have in case of repossession?

Finance Companies

Most stores and business firms do not have enough money to finance their business if they sell on an installment plan. They need their money to reinvest in replacement merchandise so they can have a rapid turnover; so they use the services of a finance company.

Sales Finance Company

A finance company that deals only in installment notes arising from sales by business firms is sometimes known as a *sales finance company*. In effect, the sales finance company purchases the installment notes from the business firm at the time of the sale, and thus immediately replenishes the merchant's cash. In some instances, the customer's payments are made to the merchant, but more often, the payments are made directly to the finance company.

The following illustrates how a sales finance company operates:

Mr. Andrews buys a refrigerator from Apex Appliance Company and owes the company $500, which, under the terms of the installment contract, is to be paid off monthly over a period of one year. Apex Appliance Company sells the installment contract to National Finance Company for $450. National Finance Company makes the collections of $500 from Mr. Andrews.

Consumer Finance Company

A finance company that makes loans directly to consumers not arising from a sale of merchandise by a business firm is sometimes referred to as a *consumer finance company*. Some finance companies serve consumers directly and also purchase installment notes from business firms. Others make installment loans which may be used to purchase various kinds of durable goods, to pay debts, to pay emergency expenses, or for home repairs.

Banks and Other Lending Agencies

Well-established business firms frequently sell directly to commercial banks installment notes that arise from the sale of merchandise to their customers. Credit unions are playing a more important role in lending money to members than was the case several years ago.

Chapter Summary

Buying on an installment plan is a frequently used method of acquiring assets which can aid in the acquisition of wealth. Through this method, you can acquire automobiles, furniture, computer systems, refrigerators, and other assets that can raise your standard of living. Installment buying requires an installment contract outlining the terms and conditions of the transaction. Finance companies may be used to finance the operation of installment plans.

CHAPTER 10

USING INSTALLMENT CREDIT

Installment credit is a convenient way to acquire certain goods when funds are not readily available to purchase on a cash basis. Even when cash is available, installment credit will allow you to buy more goods than would be the case without it. Installment credit, however, like other forms of credit, can lead to problems if not used properly. This chapter discusses certain aspects of buying on the installment plan and the wise use of installment credit. Clearly, it is closely related to the previous chapter.

> **A SUBSTANTIAL DOWN PAYMENT IS WISE**

Buying on the Installment Plan

Installment buying is a poor practice for both buyers and sellers if it is abused. Installment buying may be harmful to the consumer if he or she buys luxuries or other commodities not actually needed. There are many consumers who purchase items just because they are available on the installment plan. For example, it may be unwise to purchase expensive clothes or elaborate jewelry on the installment plan.

On the other hand, buying on an installment plan may be both economical and wise. It can be used frequently as a means of enforced saving. It should, however, be used carefully and with common sense. For example, if you are furnishing a home, the purchase of furniture on the installment plan would be justifiable if the payments could be made within the budget. Using the installment plan would be better than spending all available funds to buy cheap furnishings that would soon wear out and then have to be replaced. A writer would be justified, for example, in buying a good computer on the installment plan if it were needed in her work. If an automobile is required for work or business, installment buying is justified. Another example of using the installment buying privilege wisely is that of a medical doctor starting his or her profession, who may finance the purchase of equipment through the installment plan.

Often, the income of a family is planned in advance to such an extent that additional periodic payments on installment purchases are neither feasible nor wise. Let us consider an example. Let us assume that the monthly income of a family is $3,000, and that the family's monthly expenses are $1,750, not including housing. Assume further that payments on a mortgage, taxes, and insurance on the house in which the family lives are $825 a month; on an automobile, $250 a month; and on a refrigerator, $125 a month; making a total of $2,950 of each month's income that is committed. Under these conditions, to purchase a television set on installment would likely be unwise. The seller and the buyer of merchandise should consider together the advisability of the buyer contracting an installment debt.

Before Buying on the Installment Plan

Before you buy an item on the installment plan and accept the financing plan offered by the seller, you would do well to consider the following alternatives:

a) Buying from another seller who offers better terms
b) Paying cash from accumulated savings or waiting until you have saved enough money
c) Borrowing from a bank or another lending agency and paying cash
d) Borrowing on a life insurance policy and paying cash.

Guidelines to Follow in Making an Installment Purchase

You will find the following guidelines helpful in making an installment purchase:

1. Make a substantial down payment.
2. Pay the balance as quickly as possible.
3. Buy only durable goods that will be of value long after the final payment.
4. Don't use the full extent of your installment credit.
5. Budget your income and your expenditures to be sure that you can pay all obligations.
6. Leave a safety margin for unforeseen expenses and possible reductions in income.
7. Consider before you buy whether it is more profitable and more desirable to save your money and wait until you can pay cash.
8. Check other ways to get what you want that may be less expensive.

Benefits of Installment Buying

Buying on the installment plan has some advantages. Here are some of them:

1. Necessities may be enjoyed before the full amount of money that is required for the purchase is available.

2. Better and more substantial merchandise can sometimes be obtained by utilizing the installment plan instead of paying cash for cheap or inferior merchandise.
3. Installment buying helps many young married people who would be unable to furnish a home and start housekeeping.

Abuses of Installment Buying

The following are some of the abuses of installment buying:

1. Many people buy assets because of false pride. They are encouraged to buy more expensive assets than they can afford.
2. When the number of dealers allowing installment purchases is limited, people who wish to make installment purchases may have to accept inferior products because the grade of goods they want are not sold where they can make purchases on the installment plan.
3. People who buy on the installment plan usually pay interest at relatively high rates on the unpaid balance. Interest rates in excess of 20 percent per year are not unusual. They end up paying significantly more than they would have paid if they had purchased the merchandise for cash. If you use installment buying extensively, you will reduce your total purchasing power substantially.
4. Some people may live beyond their means because installment buying seems easy.
5. Competition for credit customers sometimes leads businesses to put customers under pressure in the hope of selling goods on easy terms.
6. Some merchants and dealers encourage buyers to use the installment plan because the finance charges produce additional income.

7. Some users of the installment plan lower their standards of food, clothing, education, and environment in order to meet obligations on installment purchases.
8. One of the greatest disadvantages is in committing oneself to future obligations. By promising to make future payments, one limits one's freedom of action and reduces one's margin of safety in financial emergencies.

It should be obvious that installment purchases should be made only on the basis of necessity and convenience after a careful study of needs and ability to pay. In general, installment buying is recommended only for accumulating worthwhile assets that will outlast the debt.

Terms of Payment

The percentage of down payment and the amount of time in which the debtor may pay vary according to the product and the policy of the finance company.

Finance Charges for Installment Service

When goods are sold on an installment plan, the seller or the one financing the sale incurs costs that would not arise with cash or charge sales. The expenses of investigating the credit standing of the purchaser, making the loan, collecting, bookkeeping, insurance, repossessing in case of delinquent payments, reselling, bad debts, and general office expenses must be covered either by increasing the sales price or by adding separate charges.

In some cases, the finance or carrying charges may seem to be unduly high; and yet in most instances, they are reasonable when the extra costs of making and collecting installment loans are considered. When dealing with a reputable business firm, finance company, or bank, it is not so much a question of whether the cost of buying on an installment plan is fair or unfair; it is a question of whether the merchandise is needed sufficiently to justify paying the amount of the finance or carrying charges.

Credit Life Insurance

Credit life insurance, also called *consumer-credit insurance*, has a connection with installment buying. This kind of insurance is short-term insurance on the life of the purchaser. Under the terms of the purchase contract and the life insurance policy, in case of the purchaser's death, the money from the insurance will be used to pay off the remaining debt under the installment plan.

Credit life insurance is inexpensive. Any reliable insurance agent can tell you what you should pay for this kind of insurance. Sometimes the cost of the insurance is included in the total cost of the installment purchase. If it is not shown as a separate item, it is sometimes difficult to determine how much is being charged. Any purchaser on an installment contract has the right to know the cost of the merchandise, the carrying charges, and all other charges that are being made.

Truth in Lending

In some jurisdictions, the law specifies that consumers have the right to know how much they are paying for the use of credit. The creditor is obliged to state exactly the monthly and annual percentage rate of charge, and in some cases, the actual dollar and cents amount of the charge as well. This *Truth in Lending* provision is clearly advantageous to consumers.

Revolving Credit

For revolving charge accounts and similar open-end credit plans offered by banks and retailers, the creditor cannot tell the consumer in advance the dollar amount of finance charges. The reason is that the creditor cannot predict how much credit the consumer will be using each month or how rapidly the consumer will be repaying for credit used. The creditor must, however, inform the consumer as to the monthly rate he or she will be charged; for example, 1 percent or 1½ percent a month. The creditor must also show what these monthly rates are on an annual basis; for example, 12 percent or 18 percent annual rate.

The consumer should note whether the creditor is charging this monthly rate on the opening unpaid balance or on the opening unpaid balance minus any payments. The creditor is required to state how the charge is being made. If the monthly rates are the same in both cases, you pay less under the latter.

Other Types of Credit

For all non-installment (single payment) and installment credit other than revolving or open-end (such as 90-day charge accounts and 6-month and 12-month loans), the creditor must show the consumer in writing the finance charges in dollar amounts as well as the monthly and annual percentage rates. If the creditor requires the consumer to buy credit life insurance, he or she must tell the consumer how much the insurance costs and include this amount in the total finance charges and the annual percentage rate. In other words, the creditor cannot charge the consumer 18 percent a year interest plus $50 or $75 extra for credit life insurance. If the creditor wants the consumer to pay the cost of the insurance in addition to the 18 percent a year, he or she must raise the monthly percentage rate to include the cost of the insurance. In this way, the consumer is in a better position to shop for credit because he or she can now compare rates as well as dollar charges among many creditors and retailers.

New Car Financing

Few people purchase new cars for cash. Typically, they own a used car which is traded in, and the value of the used car is applied as part payment for the new car. The difference between the value of the new car and the used car is generally financed by a loan of some sort. In addition to the price of the new car, the purchaser must pay all relevant taxes, and license fees, as well as auto insurance and credit life insurance. A down payment is usually required. When the balance to be financed is determined, an agreement is made to pay off the balance over a certain period of time such as 24 months or 48 months.

Balloon Payment

Some auto dealers will offer you several low monthly payments with one final large payment. For example, a dealer may offer to allow you to make 23 monthly payments of only $101.50 each with a final 24th payment of $1,650. If such an offer is made, truth in lending requires that the dealer indicate that the last payment be clearly labeled as a *balloon payment*. This should serve as a warning sign to you. If you can afford to pay only $101.50 a month for car payments for 23 months, where will you get $1,650 the 24th month? It should be plain to see that such balloon payments could get you into all kinds of credit difficulties.

Finance Charges

The creditor may not be required, under all circumstances, to show the consumer the monthly or annual percentage rate of finance charges. The creditor must, however, show the exact dollar charge. Regardless of how the terms of an installment sale plan are stated, comparisons of the actual and financial can be made provided that the finance charges and the sale price of the article, not including finance charges, are known.

In some circumstances, goods such as jewelry and clothing are offered for sale on monthly payments with "no charge for credit." However, a purchaser who offers cash usually will be able to buy the article for less than the stated price. The difference between the cash price the consumer would pay and the stated price on installments with "no charge for credit" is really the finance charge.

When making comparisons of costs of financing contemplated installment purchases, it will be well for the buyer to remember that legitimate lenders of small sums find it necessary to charge very high percentage rates to cover their actual costs of operation and to give them a profit.

Warnings on Installment Buying

It will be worth your while to heed the following warnings on installment buying.

1. Do not allow yourself to be rushed into signing a contract until you know all the facts.
2. Refuse to sign any contract if you are not given an exact duplicate copy.
3. Do not sign any contract before all the blank spaces are filled in.
4. Do not pledge any security besides the article being purchased.
5. Pay only what is shown on the copy of the contract.

The Wise Use of Installment Credit

When making wise use of installment credit, there is more to consider than simply comparing quoted percentage rates. The length of time the installment contract is to run and the deferred payment price (total of the cash price plus the finance charge) of the merchandise must be considered along with the annual percentage rate. For example, assume you were going to buy a television set for $1,000 on the installment plan. The Apex Appliance and Furniture Store offers to finance the TV set for six months at 18 percent annual rate; whereas the Best Price Electronic Store offers to finance the set for 12 months at an annual rate of only 15 percent. In comparing annual percentage rates alone, it would appear that you would pay less in finance charges at Brest Price Electronic Store. In reality, you pay less at Apex even though the annual percentage rate is three percentage points higher. See the calculations in the following table.

Table 10.1
Comparing Financing under Different Conditions

	Apex	Best Price
Amount financed	$1,000.00	$1,000.00
Length of time financed	6 months	12 months
Annual percentage rate	18%	15%
Dollar finance charge	$90.00	$150.00
Deferred payment price	$1,090.00	$1,150.00

The length of the installment contract is clearly an important factor in the amount of finance charges you have to pay. The shorter the installment contract, the less the finance charges will be in dollar terms. When shopping for credit among retailers, the wise consumer considers the length of time the installment contract is to run and the deferred payment price as well as the annual percentage rate.

Chapter Summary

Installment buying stimulates mass production and this is an important factor in our economy. A sales contract or other form of security agreement commonly provides security for the seller. Installment selling involves many extra costs that must be borne by the buyer. The finance or carrying charge is the difference between the cash price and the total cost paid under an installment contract. Buying on an installment plan costs much more than buying on a regular charge account or cash. An installment buyer should fully understand the provisions of the contract before buying.

CHAPTER 11

THE CONSUMER AND ADVERTISING

We live in a market-oriented economy and advertising is an important part of our marketing system. It has become a part of daily life. Advertising is an effective means whereby many sellers communicate with buyers. It allows buyers to get much needed information about products and services. The impact of advertising on our lives is remarkable. This chapter will help you to understand the functions and practices of advertising and how they relate to your personal interests. Advertising has an impact on wealth creation and preservation.

ADVERTISING STIMULATES CONSUMER DEMAND

Functions of Advertising

A very long time ago, before the so-called industrial revolution, production and marketing were very simple processes. Most consumers produced the goods and services they consumed, or traded with nearby acquaintances. Stores often traded goods across the counter, and very little money changed hands. The first common form of advertising was the sign of the merchant, the doctor, the blacksmith, or other professional people. In those days, mass production was unknown and mass marketing was not an essential activity.

Today, we have mass production with producers and consumers widely separated. A complicated system of transportation and communication is needed to help producers reach the consumer and to tell the consumer in distant places what the producer has to sell. Under our present economic system, advertising is essential. Advertising helps industries, and it creates employment both directly in advertising occupations and indirectly by stimulating demand for many goods and services.

In our society, mass production makes mass marketing necessary and mass marketing makes mass production possible. Without advertising, mass marketing would be impossible. Mass production, in turn, has made it possible for us to buy many goods at a greatly reduced price. In societies where producers are told what to produce and consumers can purchase only what is placed at their disposal, advertising is not so useful. In such societies, few kinds of goods are available from which to choose. Just imagine for a moment how life would be if many of the things now offered for sale were withdrawn and if we had no choice among those commodities that were made available to us!

The ultimate purpose of all advertising is to sell goods and services. Manufacturers, wholesalers, and retailers seek to achieve this objective through the several functions of advertising, which are listed below.

Many functions of advertising are beneficial to consumers as well as producers and distributors.

Major Functions of Advertising

1. Stimulate consumer demand by obtaining:
   a) Wider acceptance and greater use of products not yet universally used.
   b) Greater use of products already widely used.
   c) Wider acceptance of a commodity by consumers who have not used it.
2. Educate prospective consumers regarding:
   a) The personal benefits and satisfaction to be derived from using a particular product.
   b) Various uses of a product.
   c) Merits of a particular brand or make.
3. Inform consumers about new products, developments in present products, and changes in fashions and customs.
4. Maintain contact with consumers who, without advertising, may never know a product is available.
5. Stress exclusive features and important advantages of a product.
6. Build consumer preference for a particular brand of product, thus making it possible to price the product above competitive brands.
7. Develop large-scale distribution, thus making possible low-cost mass production.
8. Establish a trade name slogan or product image.
9. Create goodwill and develop consumer respect for the firm.
10. Obtain a list of prospective customers and prepare the way for salespeople.
11. Obtain a larger share of the business available.
12. Promote the use of one class of product as opposed to another.

Criticisms of Advertising

Although large-scale distribution and, therefore, mass production would not be possible without advertising, there are critics who believe that advertising is both unnecessary and wasteful. The fact that critics argue against advertising does not make their arguments necessarily valid. It is very easy for us to look at a disadvantage of an undesirable outcome of advertising without considering at the same time the advantages and benefits. The advertising controversy is extensive. In this chapter we shall consider a few of the benefits and the undesirable outcomes.

Advertising and Brand Switching

Critics of advertising claim that advertising that persuades consumers to switch brands among nearly identical goods is an economic waste. On the other hand, the proponents of advertising counter that advertising does more than promote brand-switching; it stimulates demand and makes possible a greater flow of goods and services that provide a higher level of living.

Advertising and Consumer Demand

Some people argue that advertising may increase the sale of some products, but it does not increase total sales. These people point out that few people need help from advertising to spend most of their income. They contend that income, employment, and psychological feelings about the future are the causes of sales. They maintain further, that there is little or no relationship between advertising and the total sales volume in the community. Proponents of advertising agree that sales are based on income, employment, and psychological feelings about the future; they contend, however, that these factors are stimulated by advertising.

Advertising and Consumer Prices

Although the cost of advertising may increase the prices of goods, there is no assurance that if there were no advertising, prices to consumers would be less. For example, suppose that two manufacturers offer computers for sale. The quality of their respective lines of computers is comparable. One manufacturer advertises widely; the other advertises very little. Yet, the prices for the computers of the manufacturer that does not advertise and the one that does are comparable. The additional cost of advertising for the one who advertises heavily may be offset by lower production costs because of greater volume of sales.

Advertising and Obsolescence

A further charge is that advertising promotes wasteful obsolescence. For example, a black cell phone is replaced with a pastel-coloured cell phone. The new cell phone is not *needed*; thus advertising promotes an economic waste. The proponents respond that all a person really *needs* is a cave, an open hearth, and an animal skin for clothes. Who should determine what a person *needs*? They argue further that the increased sales promote economic growth, which is a benefit to all.

Advertising versus Advertising Techniques

The critics of advertising seem to fall into two camps: (1) those who criticize advertising itself, and (2) those who criticize certain advertising techniques. The first group opposes all advertising and feels that expenses are wasteful. The second group favours advertising, but feels that much of today's advertising can and needs to be improved. These critics are concerned with educating consumers to demand more informative advertising. They believe that advertisers must accept high moral, social, and ethical standards. Most individual advertisers and advertising organizations actively support and laud the activities of these constructive critics.

Some of the critics of advertising appear to be too negative and offer little constructive criticism. Whether advertising is an economic plus or cost to society is not an important question in the everyday operation of business affairs. Obviously, a businessperson must let potential customers know what products are available.

The argument that advertising should be presented in good taste does seem to have merit. A problem arises, however, when one tries to define good taste. What a person considers to be good taste is strictly an individual matter. People's judgment on this issue usually rests with whether or not they agree with the action the advertiser is suggesting that the potential consumer should take. For example, many people would applaud advertisements that appeal to thrift, economy, honesty, and other similar goals but reject advertisements that appeal to fear, envy, style, and other similar appeals. There is probably no way to resolve the issue of good taste in a completely satisfactory manner.

Some Major Views of Advertising

Critics state that advertising:
1. Promotes brand-switching rather than increasing total demand and is an economic waste.
2. Increases the prices of goods and services.
3. Promotes wasteful obsolescence.
4. Appeals too much to emotions rather than to reason.
5. Controls the press.
6. Is often in poor taste and needs to be improved.

Proponents of advertising answer that advertising:
1. Increases total demand
2. Often makes lower prices possible.

3. Enhances economic and individual freedom by allowing consumers the right of "uneconomical" obsolescence.
4. Frees the presses from political control.
5. Can and should be improved.

Note: You must keep in mind that advertising is not the cause of our economic system; it is a result of our economic system.

Kinds of Advertising

Most of the advertising with which we are concerned is directed toward the ultimate consumer, that is, the person who buys for personal or household use, not for a business or a profession. Advertising addressed to or intended for the ultimate consumer is known as *consumer advertising*.

Advertising may be classified also as to its intention. If the advertising is intended to stress the benefits of a certain product, it is known as *primary advertising*. An example is the dairy industry stimulating the demand for milk through advertising. Primary advertising focuses attention on a type or a class of product, rather than on a particular brand.

Another classification of advertising as to intention is known as *selective advertising*, which attempts to persuade consumers generally to buy one brand rather than another. This is the kind of advertising that is most frequently addressed to consumers. An example of selective advertising is an auto manufacturer trying to persuade buyers to purchase its automobile rather than some other.

The Cost of Advertising

The costs of advertising are reflected in the selling prices of goods and services. Therefore, the consumer ultimately pays for advertising. It may seem unreasonable to spend $50,000 for a full-page advertisement in one issue of a magazine or $500,000 for one television program. But these advertising media respectively reach millions of people; hence the advertising cost per unit of product sold is very small. As a consumer, you should be interested in knowing how much of the dollar cost of your purchase represents advertising cost.

Consumer Analysis of Advertising

As consumers, we are exposed daily to literally hundreds of advertising messages—in newspapers and magazines, on billboards, by radio and television and the internet, and in special flyers delivered directly to our doors. Without doubt, these advertisements develop in us desires for goods and services that otherwise we would not want. This, in many aspects, is good for us, for it acquaints us with goods and services that may make living more pleasant. It is important, however, that as consumers we not only understand the motives, methods, and practices of advertisers but also that we know how to use advertising wisely in achieving our objectives. In order to use advertising wisely we must be able to analyze advertising. In Chapter 4, we discussed how advertising may be used in buying wisely. Now, we merely summarize some general guides for consumers to use in analyzing advertisements.

Consumer Guides for Analyzing Advertisements

1. Study advertisements continually to learn about new goods and services, improvements, and developments; learn to recognize trademarks, brand names, and both the manufacturers and retailers of the items you want. Use advertisements as a source of information.

2. Discover the kind of appeal used in an advertisement—emotional or reason-why. This knowledge will help you in using the advertisements wisely in making consumer choices.
3. Look for statements indicating the quality of the product advertised; if the advertisement is not adequate, seek more information from manufacturer or retailer.
4. Do not be influenced by absurd and meaningless statements and implications in advertisements. Many of them are not complimentary to your intelligence if you permit them to influence you.
5. Evaluate with great care testimonials used in advertisements; ordinarily an advertising testimonial is of little value to you.
6. Search for informative statements that explain the essential features of a product—specifications, standards, and performance.
7. Develop a pattern to follow in analyzing advertisements; you will be a more efficient and wiser consumer if analytical habits for evaluating advertisements are formed.

Benefits of Advertising

Advertising has a tremendous influence on the development of our standard of living by improving our diet, our health, our living conditions, and our comforts and conveniences. This lifting of our living standards has been brought about through constructive education and by increasing our wants for things that now seem necessary although at one time they may have seemed unnecessary. It may be true that advertising has caused us to want things that we really do not need. The consumer needs to be informed so that he or she may make intelligent decisions.

Educational Value of Advertising

The history of food consumption is a good illustration of the educational influence of advertising on our diets and general health. For example, authorities on diet long have advocated the use of orange juice, tomato juice, fresh vegetables, fresh fruits, grains and nuts in our everyday diet. Very little progress was made in establishing these foods as a part of the basic diet of most people until producers began to use advertising as a means of educating the people as to the desirability of the daily use of these foods.

The story of popularizing desirable foods is somewhat parallel to the story of popularizing the telephone, sanitary plumbing, the computer, ventilation, refrigeration, television, and many types of labour-saving devices that are now considered essential in the home. We can live without these conveniences, but our level of living would decrease greatly if we did not have them.

Product Information

Another benefit of advertising is that it acquaints consumers with the uses of certain products, particularly new ones. In many instances, consumers must be familiarized with the uses of a product before they are willing to buy. A typical example of such a product is a new computer software. People need to know the various functions that it can perform.

Social and Cultural Goals

Because advertising arouses mass desire and penetrates so deeply into our public and private lives, it potentially can be a powerful influence in formulating people's health, social, and cultural goals. For example, as our wants increase, we may demand more nutritious foods, better housing, better education, better recreational facilities, better health, and a cleaner environment.

Economic Benefits

No less important than the educational benefits of advertising are the economic benefits that it provides. As noted earlier, advertising stimulates large-scale marketing, which in turn provides an outlet for the products of mass-production methods. Thus, many products are available to consumers at reasonable prices that without advertising would not be available at all, or if they were available, the prices would be prohibitive for many consumers. We could not have many of the products we enjoy if it were not for advertising to stimulate a demand for them, thus lowering the cost of production.

Chapter Summary

The objective of advertising is to sell goods and services by stimulating demand and influencing consumers in their choices. Advertising is an essential factor in distribution; it stimulates mass production, which in turn means many more products are made available at prices consumers can afford to pay. There is disagreement as to the value of advertising to consumers. The criticisms of advertising are focused primarily on its usefulness in relation to its cost. Various kinds of advertising are intended to serve specific purposes, such as informing and educating consumers about certain products; promoting sales for an entire industry; and persuading consumers to select and buy a particular product. Advertising cost consumers in the form of slightly higher prices for goods and services. The cost of advertising paid by consumers is offset in part or wholly by the benefits consumers receive either directly or indirectly. An analysis of the motives, methods, and contents of advertisements may provide the basis for wise consumer decisions. Advertising provides valuable consumer benefits, some of which are educational or cultural, and others economic in nature.

CHAPTER 12
PROTECTION THROUGH INSURANCE

A family faces many risks that make economic and financial planning uncertain. Hurricane, flood, tornado, fire or some other catastrophe may destroy property owned by the family. Actions by members of the family may cause damage to the property of others or perhaps injury or even death. Guests of the family may suffer injury while on the family's property. These are only a few of the risks that each family must consider in making its plans. In this chapter, we analyze the ways by which the family may be protected against these risks through property and liability insurance and thus preserve wealth.

INSURANCE HELPS TO PRESERVE WEALTH

The Nature of Property and Liability Insurance

There can be little doubt that a broad need exists for property and liability insurance. In general, property and liability insurance companies are successful, and most families purchase some form of property and liability insurance. Family life has become complicated, particularly as it relates to home ownership and automobile ownership and use. Family investment in a home built up over a period of years may be destroyed in a matter of minutes by fire or tornado. Family resources may be completely wiped out by a judgment resulting from a lawsuit involving an automobile accident. The possibility that such an event might occur in a family normally would make financial and economic planning quite uncertain.

There are various ways by which a small but certain cost can be substituted for the uncertain and quite possibly large cost of a major loss. For example, groups of families could band together and agree that they would share equally in any loss sustained by one of the group members. In this case, however, the families within the group would not know when they might be called upon to share in the loss until the loss actually occurred. Thus, uncertainty would still exist.

The group of families, in order to remove this uncertainty, might agree to pay a specified amount into a fund which then could be used to pay the loss sustained by any one of the families in the group. Problems would arise, however. How much would each family pay? Who would hold the funds and bear the responsibility? How should the funds be invested? What would happen if losses were greater than the balance in the fund? How would the funds be used if no losses were sustained in a given period? An additional problem would arise from such an arrangement. Suppose that all of the families lived in one community and that a fire or a tornado destroyed the entire community. Under such conditions, it is obvious that the funds would not be adequate to pay for all of the losses.

Property and liability insurance companies are organized in such a way that they can satisfactorily handle all of the problems listed in the previous paragraph. These insurance companies receive relatively small payments from large numbers of individuals and families in many different communities, invest these funds, and pay for losses sustained by the member families. The insurance company takes a calculated risk, while each property owner pays a certain amount each year so that if a family's home is burned, that family will be paid for the loss by the insurance company.

Some Definitions

Insurance then can be defined as a promise of reimbursement in the case of specific potential future losses in exchange for a periodic payment. The insurance agreement is a form of contract. An insurance contract is called a *policy*. The person who buys an insurance policy pays periodically what is called a *premium*, and is referred to as the *policyholder* or the i*nsured*. The party from whom the policyholder buys the insurance and who agrees to pay the loss is called the *insurer* or *underwriter*. *Risk* is the possibility of loss. *Face value* is the amount of insurance stated in the contract; *cash value* is the actual market value of the property destroyed. Cash value may be greater or less than the face value of the contract.

Property Insurance

The greatest risks of loss to a family or individual usually are associated with the ownership and operation of a home and an automobile. Therefore, we shall consider the different types of property and liability insurance as they relate to the home and the automobile. In this section we deal with property insurance, deferring liability insurance for the next section. Insurance for the automobile will be treated separately in a later section.

Homeowners must consider the many risks that they face and the possible losses that they may incur. They must consider the possible loss of their homes, the contents, and other personal property. They must consider possible losses arising from lawsuits resulting from personal injury to guests. While each of these risks can be insured against separately, insurance companies have developed insurance policies that insure against groups of perils. Such policies are called *homeowners policies*.

The homeowners' policy is available to owner-occupants of one- and two-family private residences. Although the policy insures against many perils, there is only one policy and only one premium payment with which to be concerned. In addition, the package of insurance ordinarily costs significantly less than that of separately purchased coverages.

Under a typical homeowners' policy, not all perils are covered. *Personal property* is generally covered along with the house. Personal property includes household contents and other personal belongings used, owned, worn, or carried by the family. Pets are not usually included as personal property. It is the responsibility of the policyholder to make sure that he or she knows exactly what is and what is not covered. The policyholder should read the policy carefully. It is possible to buy additional insurance to cover those items that are excluded from the package.

Amount of Coverage

If you happen to be a homeowner, you should carry enough property insurance, but not too much. The amount of insurance that you should purchase is determined by the replacement cost of the home. Replacement costs usually are determined through an appraisal by a competent appraiser.

Assume that the appraisal indicates that $400,000 of insurance should be carried on the house. This amount then determines the amount of other property coverages included in the homeowners policy. These coverages might be as follows:

Dwelling..$400,000
Personal property (not otherwise covered)
(40 percent of dwelling)...................................... 160,000
Additional living expense (20 percent of dwelling)......... 80,000

Need for Inventory

An inventory of personal property is desirable and necessary in the event of loss. This inventory serves as the basis for making claims and eliminates the need for depending on memory. Some homeowners keep accurate listings of their personal property; others photograph each room in the home. Of course, the inventory or photographs must be kept in a safe, fireproof place. An illustration of a portion of a household inventory record is shown in Table 12.1.

Table 12.1
A Portion of a Household Inventory Record

Kitchen, Utility Room

No.	Article	Year Bought	Original Cost	Present Cash Value
	Chairs, Tables, Stools			
	Draperies, Rugs			
	Dishes, Glassware			
	Refrigerator			
	Range			
	Dishwasher			
	Washing Machine			
	Dryer			

No.	Article	Year Bought	Original Cost	Present Cash Value
	Waste Disposer			
	Electrical Appliances (Vacuum Cleaner, Toaster, Coffeemaker, Fry-Skillet, etc.)			
	Kitchen Equipment (Foodstuffs, Supplies, Cutlery, Utensils, etc.)			
	Kitchen Cabinets			
	↓	↓	↓	↓

Note: Some insurance companies provide policyholders with blank inventory forms that they can easily complete.

Liability Insurance

People may injure themselves or may suffer damage to their property while on the premises of a homeowner. In addition, the actions of the family may result in injury to other persons or damage to their property either on the premises of the homeowner or away. The members of the family may become personally liable for claims arising as a result of these situations.

The liability insurance portion of a homeowners policy generally protects the family against claims in three areas:

1. Comprehensive personal liability
2. Medical payments
3. Physical damage to the property of others

Let us examine each of these areas, beginning with comprehensive personal liability.

Comprehensive Personal Liability

Coverage under a comprehensive-personal-liability policy protects the homeowner against claims arising from bodily injury to others or damage to their property. No claim is paid by the insurance company under this provision unless it has been established that the insured is legally liable. A guest in the home might fall down a basement stairway, break a leg, and then file suit for damages. Under this provision, the insurance company would represent the homeowner in court, pay the cost of defending the homeowner, and pay the damages, if any, up to the limits of the policy.

Medical Payments

Coverage under a medical-payments provision in a homeowners policy protects the homeowner from accidental injury claims arising from action of the homeowner, and members of his or her family either on or off the homeowner's property. The insurance company pays the claims of the injured party, regardless of who is at fault, for the cost of medical and surgical services incurred, usually within one year of the accident.

Physical Damage to the Property of Others

A clause providing coverage for physical damage to the property of others protects the homeowner and his or her family when any member of the family damages someone's property. For example, the homeowner's lawn mower might throw a stone through a neighbor's window. Such damages are paid up to the limit of the policy. Coverage is provided whether the act is committed on the property of the homeowner or off and whether or not the homeowner is at fault.

Determinants of the Cost of Property and Liability Insurance

There are several factors that determine the cost of property and liability insurance, but they are all related to the degree of risk to which the homeowner is exposed. Here we consider the following factors:

- Geographical location
- Availability of water supply for fire fighting
- Proximity to the local fire department
- Type of construction of the home
- Smoking habit of the homeowner
- The presence of smoke detectors

Geographical Location

If the property is located in an area where fires are prevalent or where crime to property is rampant, the cost of property and liability insurance is likely to be higher than an area where fires are rare or where crime to property is extremely low. This is due to the higher risk involved.

Availability of Water Supply for Fire Fighting

Other things being equal, the cost of insuring a property that is close to a fire hydrant or other sources of water is lower than one that is far from water. The reason for the difference in cost is that in the event of a fire, the probability of the house that is close to the fire hydrant being destroyed by the fire is lower than that associated with the house that is far from water sources.

Proximity to the Local Fire Department

In the event of a fire at a property that is located in close proximity to the local fire department, fire fighters can get to the property to put out the fire in a relatively short time. Many properties that have been destroyed by fire could have been saved had they been located in close proximity to a fire department.

Type of Construction of the Home

The material from which the home is constructed is an important factor in determining the cost of property insurance. A building of concrete blocks and bricks is less susceptible to fire, hurricane, and other hazards than one that is constructed with wood. Hence, insurance for the latter is more expensive than that for the former.

Smoking Habit of the Homeowner

Smoking in bed is a prime cause of fires in homes. Thus, smokers pay a higher cost for insurance than do non-smokers. Of course, knowledge of the health risks of smoking and laws against smoking in certain areas have significantly reduced the number of smokers.

The Presence of Smoke Detectors

The absence of smoke detectors from homes and defective smoke detectors have led to many fires. If a fire does occur, the sound of the noise from the smoke detector serves as an early warning, so that prompt action can be taken before the fire gets out of control. The presence of smoke detectors in homes reduces the cost of property insurance.

Automobile Insurance

No automobile owner or driver should be without automobile insurance. In fact, some jurisdictions require that automobile owners and drivers have certain types of insurance to protect others from loss. Family economic security is very uncertain unless the perils arising from automobile ownership are insured. The owner or operator of an automobile should consider the following types of coverage:

1. Bodily injury liability
2. Property damage liability
3. Medical payments
4. Comprehensive physical damage
5. Collision
6. Protection against uninsured motorists

These six coverages may be purchased separately; but, as in the case of the homeowners policy, it is more common to purchase the six coverages as a package. Each of the coverages will be discussed separately in the following pages.

Bodily Injury Liability

All members of the family are protected by this insurance as well as those who drive the insured's car with his or her permission. In addition, members of the insured's family are covered while driving another person's car if the owner has given his or her permission. This insurance protects the insured against claims or suits of people injured or killed by the insured's automobile. In some jurisdictions, there are laws indicating the minimum amount of this coverage that must be carried.

Property Damage Liability

All members of the family and all those driving the family car with permission are covered by this policy provision. Members of the family are covered even while driving someone else's car as long as they have permission from the owner. This coverage protects the insured whenever his or her automobile damages the property of others.

Both bodily injury and property damage coverage are absolutely essential for the automobile owner. The perils that face the automobile owner are too great to risk without adequate insurance coverage. In purchasing this coverage, it should be remembered that large amounts of coverage cost relatively less than smaller amounts. Thus, it is often possible for you to double your coverage with only a slight increase in premium cost.

Medical Payments Coverage

This coverage is similar to that discussed under the homeowners policy. However, this coverage applies only to the operation of an automobile, and it covers all members of the family and any guests while riding in the insured car. Under the provisions of this coverage, the insurance company agrees to pay all *reasonable* expenses incurred for medical, surgical, X-ray, and dental services, up to the limits set in the policy. It may even include ambulance services, hospital services, nursing services, and funeral services.

Needless to say, medical payments coverage is particularly important for families with children and for families who transport other children as in a school carpool.

Comprehensive Physical Damage Insurance

This insurance coverage protects the insured against possible loss due to damage to the car or if it is stolen. However, damage due to collision is not covered. Causes of damage covered include fire, lightning, flood, and windstorm. Glass breakage is covered under this insurance. Since this type of insurance is relatively inexpensive, most automobile owners include it in their coverage. The cost of replacing one windshield very probably would be greater than total premium payments on comprehensive insurance for two or three years.

Collision Insurance

Collision insurance coverage protects the insured against loss arising from damage to his or her own car as a result of collision. This is the most expensive insurance coverage among those discussed, primarily because of the many minor accidents that require expensive body and paintwork. The car owner can reduce the cost of this type of insurance by purchasing a deductible policy. In the event of damage, the insurance company would pay only the amount of the loss in excess of the deductible amount. Since the car owner has a large investment in a new car, he or she should purchase collision insurance on a new car. As the car gets older and its value decreases, the owner should weigh the cost of this insurance coverage against the potential loss. For example, there would be little reason to carry $250 deductible collision insurance on a car with a value of $600.

Costs for collision insurance vary widely from one geographic area to another. They also vary within an area according to driver classification. Typically, young, unmarried male drivers pay relatively high rates. If the car owner finances the purchase of the automobile, he or she will be required to purchase collision insurance as well as other coverages.

Protection against Uninsured Motorists

This insurance coverage is designed to protect the family against risks due to injury by hit-and-run drivers and uninsured drivers. It covers the insured to the extent that he or she would have been covered if the uninsured driver had been insured or if the hit-and-run driver had been identified. Therefore, the insured cannot collect from the insurance company unless the uninsured motorist is legally liable. The coverage is limited to the amount of liability required under the financial responsibility laws of the various jurisdictions. The cost of this insurance is relatively low.

Determinants of the Cost of Automobile Insurance

Accidents involving automobiles are frequent, and as the number of automobiles increases, so does the probability of accidents. The cost of repairs is quite high. Automobile insurance rates must reflect these costs. The insurance rates charged by automobile insurance companies are based for the most part on what the companies have had to pay out in claims over the past few years. The following are the main factors affecting the cost of automobile insurance:

The Practices of the Companies in Accepting Risks An insurance company, by being very selective in choosing the owners and drivers that it will insure, can have lower costs and lower premium rates than a company that is not so selective.

The Experience of the Company A second factor affecting the cost of automobile insurance relates to the experience of the company. More accidents occur in urban areas than in rural areas. More occur in some urban areas than in others. Therefore, comparable coverage in one city may cost more or less than in another.

The Cost of Automobile Repairs A third factor affecting the cost of automobile insurance is the cost of automobile repairs. Some cars are more expensive and more difficult to repair than others.

The Automobile Driver A fourth factor affecting automobile rates is the driver. Statistics indicate that drivers of a certain age and sex have more or fewer accidents than others. Drivers are classified as to risk, and insurance rages are based on these risks.

We as automobile drivers and consumers of automobile insurance services should remember that automobile insurance rates are based on the experience of the insurance companies. The more automobile accidents drivers have and the more claims they file, the higher rates will be.

Selecting an Insurance Company

Many good insurance companies exist. Since most readers may not be expert enough to determine what a good insurance company is, they have to rely upon the reputations of companies.

The rates of some companies may be slightly lower than those of others, but rates are not the only basis for selecting an insurance company. Above all else, you want an insurance company that will protect you and settle claims in a reasonable manner. An insurance company that will not pay honest claims promptly and without lawsuits is not one with which you would want to insure. One of the best ways to select a company is, therefore, to inquire among your friends in order to discover the reputation of the company as to its methods of doing business and settling claims.

Many families rely on their insurance agents rather than on their knowledge of insurance companies. By selecting an agent in whom they have complete confidence, they are in effect depending on his or her judgment for the selection of the insurance company. A good agent will always act on behalf of the policyholder and will render many extra services.

Chapter Summary

Property and liability insurance is possible through small payments collected from many people to pay unexpected losses that may occur to any one of the policyholders, and rates are determined from past experience. The homeowners policy is the most economical way of insuring the homeowner against the perils of home ownership. It is absolutely essential for the family to carry adequate automobile insurance. The family should purchase its property and liability insurance from a company it knows to be reputable and fair or from an agent in whom the family has complete confidence.

CHAPTER 13

LIFE AND HEALTH INSURANCE

Consumers need to understand financial problems that result from a death in the family, accident, or disabling illness. In this chapter, we discuss how life and health insurance may help to solve these problems. We will discuss the meaning of life insurance, the different types of life insurance, the characteristics of life insurance policies, health insurance, and insurance against loss of income.

> LIFE INSURANCE CAN BE A MEANS OF SAVING

Meaning of Life Insurance

Life insurance serves several purposes. First, it may provide a cash reserve or a continuous monthly income in case of the death of a member of a family, especially the death of the primary wage earner. Second, life insurance may provide funds for future use, such as financing a college education, meeting financial emergencies, or providing either income or a cash reserve for use in retirement years. Finally, many people make regular premium payments on life insurance as a means of saving. Thus, life insurance has many uses both if the primary wage earner dies and if he or she lives.

Life insurance is a voluntary financial plan whereby an individual makes periodic payments to an insurance company. The company in turn repays the individual or the one whom he or she designates as his or her beneficiary at a specified future time or upon the occurrence of certain events such as death, accident, or disability.

Types of Ordinary Life Insurance

There are many types of life insurance contracts, usually referred to as *policies*. Some of them are simple; others involve a combination of elements that cannot be explained without considerable detail. The following are the basic types of ordinary life insurance:

- Term insurance
- Straight life insurance
- Limited-payment life insurance
- Endowment insurance
- Combination life insurance
- Annuity contracts

These types of policies are explained below.

Term Insurance

Term insurance covers a specified period of time and is usually obtained to cover a specific need. For example, if a person has a debt that he or she expects to repay in ten years, provided he or she lives, that person can buy a ten-year term policy for the amount of the indebtedness. This insurance will pay the debt in case he or she dies.

Term insurance is often referred to as "pure insurance" because it provides protection only. It does not have a cash-surrender or a loan value. One of the major advantages of term insurance is its initial low cost for a young person compared with that of other types of insurance. Term insurance makes it possible for a young person to acquire more insurance coverage at the time protection is needed but when income is too low to buy permanent protection.

The most common periods covered by term insurance are five years and ten years, but it may cover any period of years. Term insurance policies that are convertible into other types of contracts that provide protection over longer periods of years and that involve the accumulation of reserves may be purchased. For instance, a person may wish a large amount of protection at a low cost while the children are of school or college age. After the children have been educated, the person may then convert the term insurance into some other type of insurance at a higher cost without another physical examination.

Straight Life Insurance

The basic life insurance policy that provides protection over a long period of years is called *straight life insurance*. It is occasionally called *ordinary life insurance* to mean all forms of standard life insurance policies except those classified as industrial or group insurance.

If a person has dependents and is anxious to provide primarily for their protection in the event of his or her death, the straight life plan is ideal. The premium rate is lower than that for any other type of permanent insurance. The policyholder has a loan or a cash-surrender value in the policy. The insured person may continue paying premiums for the entire length of his or her life or at some specific age (such as 100) at which time he or she is paid the face value of the insurance policy.

Limited-Payment Life Insurance

A *limited-payment life insurance* contract is the same as a straight life contract except that premiums are paid for a limited time, such as 10, 20, or 30 years, instead of for life. Because premiums are paid only for a limited time, the rates are somewhat higher than for straight life insurance. When these premiums have been paid, the insurance policy is said to be fully paid. If the face value of the policy is, for example, $50,000, the insurance company will pay this amount whenever death occurs.

Endowment Insurance

The company that issues an endowment policy agrees to pay a definite sum of money at a specified time to the insured, or, in the event of death, to the beneficiary of the insured. An endowment policy costs more than a limited-payment for an equivalent number of years. The face amount is available, however, as cash at the time of death or at the end of the period.

An endowment policy is an excellent means of accumulating a definite amount for a future need. Short-term endowments for periods of from 10 to 20 years are ideal to create sums of money that will be needed to educate children, to start a child in some particular profession or business, to purchase a home, or to repay a debt.

It is often desirable to obtain a long-term endowment policy so that the money will become available at about the age of 65 or later. At this stage in life the insured may have reduced income, having reached retirement or a period of reduced earning power. If the policy matures at that time, its face value will be available to provide additional income during the later years of life.

Combination Life Insurance

Many contracts involve combinations of various types of life insurance. For example, one particular type of combination policy provides a low rate for the first four or five years and a higher rate in later years. The same insurance plan would be carried out if an individual purchased a term insurance policy and then, at the end of four or five years, converted in into a straight life, a limited-payment life, or an endowment policy.

Annuity Contracts

An *annuity* is a sum of money payable yearly. Many people purchase an annuity by turning over to an insurance company a specified sum of money as a single premium or in regular payments. In return for this sum of money, the insurance company agrees to pay a specified monthly or yearly income over a definite period of years or until the death of the insured. The cash value that has accumulated in a permanent type of life insurance policy can be taken as income over a period of years by the insured. This, in effect, is an annuity. In this way a specified income is assured to the insured or to his or her beneficiary after his or her death.

There are many types of annuity contracts. However, the principal feature of an annuity is guaranteed income starting at a certain age. Therefore, through an annuity one may, during one's earning years, provide for an income after retirement.

Other Kinds of Life Insurance

The types of life insurance discussed up to this point are called ordinary insurance. There are some other types—industrial and group—that may have some of the features of ordinary insurance but also have other characteristics.

Industrial Insurance

Industrial insurance is the type of insurance that requires small weekly, semi-monthly, or sometimes monthly, payments. It is commonly sold to the industrial or wage-earning group. The payment each week is usually quite small.

Industrial insurance serves essentially the following useful purposes. It reaches many people who would otherwise not buy any insurance; it teaches these people to save and to guard against unfavorable events or circumstances; it enables many people who are not insurable under other plans to obtain insurance. Unfortunately, most of the people who buy industrial insurance policies do not continue them until they mature or until benefits might be received at the time of death.

The current trend of insurance companies is not to offer new industrial policies to policyholders but only to service those already started.

Group Insurance

Group insurance is usually used to protect the workers of a common employer. Under this plan, many employees can be insured through one policy and without medical examination. The cost is determined by an analysis of the group and is based on the losses indicated by the ages, environment, occupation, and general health of the members. The rates may be increased or decreased, but they are usually low. Employers pay part or all of the premiums. Group insurance is also sold to members of labor unions or other associations.

There are two types of group insurance: one is *group term insurance* that does not build up any cash value; the other is *group permanent life insurance* that does accumulate a cash value.

When employees who are covered under a group policy leave the employment through which they have been insured, their protection stops. They sometimes may convert their term insurance to a regular policy within a specified time and will then pay annual premiums determined by their ages at that time. If the employees were covered under a group permanent policy, they are usually entitled to the fully paid-up protection that has been purchased to date. Sometimes under group permanent insurance plans, individual certificates are issued that resemble individual life policies. In the case of permanent insurance, these policies may be converted to regular individual policies and continued by the former employee.

One disadvantage of group term insurance is that the premium rates for a person of retirement age increase sharply or the amount of the term insurance available to the retired employee is reduced sharply.

Characteristics of Life Insurance Policies

There are many different kinds of insurance contracts. Anyone considering a life insurance policy should understand the features of life insurance policies.

Insurance as a Form of Saving

If you are considering insurance as a form of saving, you must compare it with at least two other forms of saving: (a) the deposit of savings in a bank and (b) the purchase of government bonds. There are advantages to each of the three forms. Certain types of insurance policies, such as the endowment policy, are in reality insurance plus the savings element. Of course, insurance savings do not accumulate as rapidly as bank savings because, in the case of insurance, a part of each payment is used to provide for the protection involved.

Bank savings offer no financial protection beyond the amount of the deposits and the accumulated interest. These savings can, however, be readily withdrawn. If funds are borrowed on an insurance policy, interest must be paid. Government bonds offer an excellent medium of savings because they can be bought in small denominations, pay a fair rate (although usually lower than banks), and can be converted to cash.

Incontestable Clause

If you are a purchaser of life insurance, you should understand the meaning of the *incontestable clause* in your policy. The essence of such a clause is that, if the insurance company and its agents have not discovered within a specified time that you intentionally or unintentionally made misstatements of fact with regard to diseases or other information required in the application, the insurance company cannot contest the validity of the policy. In other words, if any error has been made, it is the responsibility of the insurance company to discover such a fact within the time limit specified in the incontestable clause.

Non-forfeiture Values

All life insurance companies provide a choice of *non-forfeiture values* to a policyholder who stops paying premiums on any policy except term insurance. These choices are cash value, extended term insurance, and paid-up insurance. The following is an explanation of these non-forfeiture values:

1. Each policy states the cash value, which is the amount of money that will be paid to the insured if the policy is cancelled. The cash value is stated in his or her contract as required by law.
2. If the insured wishes to continue the maximum amount of insurance protection without paying premiums, he or she may accept *extended term insurance*. This continues the face value of the policy for as long as the accumulated cash value will pay the premium.
3. Under the *paid-up insurance* plan, the cash value is used to buy a reduced amount of fully paid insurance.

Paying Premiums

Premiums are due on the date mentioned in the policy. Life insurance policies generally allow what is called a grace period. This is a period ranging of several specified days after the date the premium is due. If the premium is paid during this grace period, there is no penalty to the policyholder. The policy lapses if the premium is not paid during the grace period. This means the termination of the contract and the loss of protection unless the policy has a value that will automatically continue part or all of the insurance for a time. However, if you stop payments of premiums, you may reinstate your insurance policy provided you have not surrendered your policy for a cash settlement. In order to reinstate it, you must meet all requirements of any person buying a new policy. You will be required to take a new physical examination and pay all the overdue premiums with interest or the increase in cash value. Some policies also have other requirements for reinstatement.

Changing the Beneficiary

When anyone buys a life insurance policy, that person names a beneficiary, or the policy becomes payable to the estate upon his or her death. The *estate* is the term used to describe the money and other property left by a deceased person to be distributed according to a will or the relevant laws. If you decide to change your beneficiary, you may do so at any time by filling out forms provided by the insurance company. This may be dome provided you have reserved this right in your policy. If you have not reserved the right to change your beneficiary, you must get the written consent of the original beneficiary before naming a new one.

Assigning the Policy

If you have reserved the right to change the beneficiary to your life insurance policy, it can be assigned as security for a loan. Banks will lend money on some life insurance policies provided the policy is assigned to the bank as security for the loan.

Extra Benefits

Some life insurance contracts have provisions whereby it is not necessary to pay premiums if the insured becomes permanently disabled. This provision is called a *premium waiver*. Other policies provide twice the amount of death benefit if the insured dies as the result of an accident instead of from natural causes. This provision in an insurance policy is generally referred to as the *double indemnity clause*.

Each company sets its own standard practices, provided these practices are according to the law. The clauses in policies of the same type issued by one company in different jurisdictions may not always be alike, however, for the various clauses must conform to the laws of the jurisdictions in which the company operates and in which policies are issued.

Health Insurance

Health care is very expensive, and illness can devastate a family. The main purpose of health insurance is to protect the family against the financial problems that might arise as a result of the illness of any member of the family or an accident to any member of the family. In regular life insurance policies, special clauses are sometimes included to protect against financial loss resulting from accidents and sickness. One or all of the following may be covered by health insurance:

- ♦ Hospital expense
- ♦ Surgical expense

- General medical expense
- Major medical expense
- Loss of income

Hospital Expense Insurance

Hospital expense insurance provides benefits equal to all or part of the cost of a hospital room and board. There is usually a limit to the number of days that are covered under the policy. The family's choice of a room, of course, determines whether the hospital expense insurance is sufficient. The policy may also provide benefits such as X-ray services, medications, and operating room services. It is worth noting that hospital expense insurance is the most widely used form of health insurance in many countries.

Surgical Expense Insurance

This category of health insurance provides for payment of surgical costs according to a schedule of fees payable for each type of surgery. The schedule of fees is based on the nature of the operation. For example, the surgeon's fee for a tonsillectomy (an operation to remove the tonsils) may be $3,500 and his or her fee for a more complicated procedure may be several thousands of dollars. Surgical expense insurance is a widely used form of health insurance.

General Medical Expense Insurance

General medical expense insurance provides benefits payable toward the expenses of calls made by doctors at the hospital or at home, or for visits by the patient to the doctor's office. Details of the coverage are spelled out in the contract.

Major Medical Expense Insurance

Major illness or serious accident can be quite costly. The purpose of major medical expense insurance is to cover the major portion of the costs incurred as the result of major illness or serious accident. Major illness and serious accidents may result in expenses amounting to hundreds of thousands of dollars.

Major medical insurance is designed to begin where hospital, surgical, and general medical insurance end. For this reason, most major medical policies have a deductible clause. Thus, the insured person may be required to pay the first $1,000 or any cost not covered by the basic policies. In addition, he or she may have to pay 20 to 25 percent of any amount exceeding the first $1,000. In insurance jargon, this is known as *coinsurance*. It helps to keep down the costs of the insurance by discouraging the insured from incurring charges for unnecessary services during his or her illness and recuperation.

Loss-of-Income Insurance

An individual could suffer a loss of income because of illness of accident. Loss-of-income insurance is designed to replace all or part of that lost income. Premiums are based on the amount of income that is to be replaced and the length of time for which payments will be made. Typically, there is a waiting period (perhaps days or weeks) before benefits are payable. Families with loss-of-income insurance are assured that they will have income in the event of prolonged illness. Whether or not a family should carry loss-of-income insurance depends on factors such as the sick leave provisions of the wage earner's job, workers' compensation provisions, and other factors.

Chapter Summary

A life insurance policy is a contract. Term insurance is usually the least expensive form of life insurance, but it does not accumulate a cash value. Straight life insurance is the least expensive form of *permanent* insurance. Endowment insurance builds the greatest cash value. Health insurance protects a family or individual against financial loss resulting from illness or accident. The most common types of health insurance are hospital expense, surgical expense, and general medical expense. Every family in moderate financial circumstances should consider hospital and surgical expense insurance coverage. Major medical insurance protects against the major portion of the cost of major illness or accident. The family should insure against only the most serious losses; minor medical expenses should be taken care of as part of the regular family financial plan.

CHAPTER 14

BUYING LIFE INSURANCE

Insurance plays an important role in preserving wealth. Without the right type of insurance, the family fortune can rapidly disappear. It is necessary to develop an insurance program that includes the father, the mother, and the children. Proper coverage of family risks makes it necessary to select a sound insurance company, a good agent, and appropriate policies. In this chapter, we discuss and analyze the problems that the family must solve in developing a good insurance program.

> **DEAL ONLY WITH A REPUTABLE AGENT**

Selecting an Insurance Company

On what basis should you select an insurance company? When making a decision about the insurance company from which you should purchase a life insurance policy, you should carefully study the following:

- Operating success

- Reputation
- Financial soundness

A good idea is to contact the company and request a copy of its annual report. In addition, you can check the internet for insurance company ratings. Standard and Poor's (S & P) is a good place to start. That company provides information on the financial strength of insurance companies. Also, you may know people who do business with the life insurance company and some of them may be willing to tell you of their experiences.

As is the case with other types of purchases, you should plan to buy insurance from the company that offers the best value. This means, therefore, that costs as well as provisions of policies should be thoroughly studied and considered.

Comparing Costs of Policies

In comparing the cost of a policy of one company with that of another, only equivalent contracts should be considered. Apples should not be compared with oranges. It is necessary to exercise caution since policies that may appear to be identical often differ significantly in meaningful ways such as in non-forfeiture benefits, and in settlement values.

Some life insurance companies may pay dividends to policyholders out of their profits. Policies issued by these companies are known as *participating policies*. Other life insurance companies do not pay dividends to policyholders and, therefore, their policies are not participating. Under a participating policy, a policyholder may receive an annual dividend based upon the amount of premiums he or she paid. The amount of the premium less the dividend received is the net cost of the premium on his or her policy. Under a non-participating policy, the amount of premium paid is the net cost of the policy per year. You must realize that the payment of the dividend is not guaranteed. In any given year, the company may decide not to pay out any dividends.

The cost of an insurance policy differs among companies, but competition tends to restrict these differences. The difference in cost between insurance bought on the participating as compared with non-participating basis can be measured accurately only over a long period of time.

Selecting an Agent

An insurance agent represents the company to the client. Many of them are honourable and consider the insurance needs of their clients. The purchaser of insurance should bear in mind, however, that some insurance agents may be so eager to sell that they may make recommendations sometimes just to please the person who is buying the insurance, even though it may not be the best possible recommendation. The buyer of insurance must therefore learn the basic principles of insurance so that he or she may judge the merits of an insurance agent's recommendations.

When selecting an insurance agent, you are really selecting both a company and an agent. This may present problems. However, you can compare rates. You should then inquire among your friends for their recommendations of agents and companies with whom they have done business. This is probably one of the best ways to find an agent who can serve you well.

Many agents study life insurance through correspondence or online, and by taking courses in schools. The purpose of such study is to help the agent learn the fundamental principles of life insurance, the nature of the various contracts and policies, and the principles of insurance program planning for an individual or family. Upon the completion of the course of study, the agents take an examination. If they are successful in passing the examination, they are awarded the relevant certificate which certifies that they are sufficiently informed about insurance and are capable of giving sound advice about insurance planning.

Factors to Consider in Selecting an Insurance Company

1. Compare rates, including dividends, among companies.
2. Select only a company that has a good reputation and is financially sound.
3. Deal only with a reputable agent.
4. In comparing policies, do not compare cost alone. Make sure that the policies are identical in every respect.
5. Bear in mind that the dividend rate or other factors will not necessarily remain the same in the future.

Using the Agent

A reliable agent who is working for a reputable company will give sound advice to prospective purchasers of insurance. In applying for an insurance policy, the applicant is usually required to indicate the amount of insurance he or she already owns. This information is useful in giving the insurance company an opportunity to determine whether the applicant is justified in purchasing additional insurance. If additional insurance is needed, and if its purchase will fit into the budget, the insurance agent can help you select the proper kind.

A good life insurance agent is one who not only has an adequate knowledge of life insurance but who also has learned how to help people determine their insurance needs and to fit an insurance program to those needs. If you want to obtain the best use of your insurance dollars, you must find such an agent and trust him or her as you would your physician or lawyer. Only then can the agent really help you. Such an agent can help you:

1. Plan insurance protection to fit your needs and those of your dependents.
2. Design an insurance program that will include the savings you want for your retirement and for specific purposes such as travelling and for the education of your children.
3. Fit the purchasing of policies to your present and future income.
4. Revise your insurance program periodically and help you build onto it, as circumstances change.

Planning a Life Insurance Program

Every family should consider an insurance program at the time of marriage when the family is formed and then modify the program as changing conditions warrant. The following are the three main questions that should be answered in insurance planning:

1. How much life insurance does the family need?
2. What kind of financial protection through insurance is needed?
3. How much insurance can the family afford?

You should consider the insurance needs of the family in relation to the family income. You should consult the insurance agent at this point so that he or she can recommend policies that are suitable to meet the needs of the family. For example, if a family member dies, money should be available to meet such an emergency.

There should also be a fund of cash available so that the family can operate until certain adjustments are made to the family budget. There may be a debt on the house. One insurance policy may be needed to pay off that mortgage in case of death. Some insurance policies are purchased for the specific purpose of providing funds to send children to university in case of the death of the father or mother.

Insurance designed to provide income for living expenses for the family should be arranged so that payments are made monthly for a certain period of years or for an indefinite period of years.

Life insurance programs should be designed primarily to replace income lost to a family when the main income earner dies. The other parent should be covered by life insurance. Upon the death of one spouse, the surviving spouse is faced immediately with burial expenses and the possible need to pay for child care for a certain period of time.

Except for certain sums of money that may be needed at the time of death, the proceeds of the insurance should be looked upon as an income that will be paid regularly under some prescribed plan to the family of the deceased spouse. A total of $50,000 may sound like a large sum of money, and it really is, as you will find when you try to save that amount. But at 2% interest, $50,000 will provide only $1000 a year of interest income. Life insurance policies can be arranged to provide monthly cheques consisting of both principal and interest instead of a lump-sum payment or instead of interest alone.

Life Insurance Expenditures and Personal Income

A question that is frequently asked is: How much of personal income should be spent in purchasing life insurance? The answer really depends on several factors such as income, family situation, individual assets, investments, and so on. When a married person's income is small, he or she needs insurance because some protection is needed for dependents. The amount that a person sets aside for insurance should be budgeted in the same manner as other expenditures. In general, as a person's income increases, the amount spent for insurance should also increase.

The amount of insurance that should be bought is a special problem for each individual. It must be determined by considering income, necessary expenditures, the accumulation of a cash savings fund, and the care of dependents.

The percentage of income spent on insurance in any particular case will depend on the following factors:

- Your level of living
- Your sense of responsibility
- The cost of living
- The number of dependents you have
- The type of insurance you buy.

It is entirely possible that a person with no particular family responsibilities may feel that he or she does not need much insurance. He or she may prefer to invest his or her money in other ways.

Insurance as a Source of Future Income

We end this chapter by considering insurance as a source of future income. Insurance can provide future income in the following ways:

1. By creating a cash estate, which will be invested to provide an income.
2. Buy buying sufficient insurance to yield a fixed amount of income for life after a certain age.
3. By arranging with the insurance company to use the proceeds of the insurance policy for paying a fixed income to dependents after the death of the insured.

Let us briefly examine each of these options in turn, beginning with the creation of a cash estate.

Creating a Cash Estate for Investment

Under this plan, you can consider your insurance and your other savings in computing the amount of income that will be available.

Suppose, for example, that you have planned your insurance program so that the cash proceeds available at your contemplated retirement age of 65 will amount to $50,000. If this amount is invested at 4%, it will pay an annual income of $1,000. This income, along with income from other sources such as savings, investment, etc.), will represent the amount that you may expect for use after you retire, provided you do not spend part of the principal.

Buying Sufficient Insurance to Yield Income

Under this option, it is possible for you to make a contract with an insurance company whereby the proceeds of insurance are to provide: (a) a guaranteed income for life or (b) a guaranteed income for life with a cash settlement if death occurs within a certain period. Some settlement options guarantee payments for a certain number of years and for life thereafter if you live longer. If you do not live beyond the fixed number of years, your beneficiary will receive a specified cash settlement.

Arranging for the Proceeds to Provide Fixed Income for Dependents

Under this option, you can make arrangements for the proceeds of your insurance to be left with the insurance company after your death so that your dependents can be paid a fixed income for a specified number of years.

Buying insurance should be just one part of the plan of building up savings and providing for the protection of dependents. In deciding how much insurance to buy, you should consider your entire financial program. Your life insurance agent should be quite helpful in arranging the details of adequate protection and proper payments.

Chapter Summary

The reputation, success, and financial soundness of insurance companies are important factors in selecting a company. Select an insurance agent who represents a sound, acceptable company and who is competent through experience and training to advise you about your insurance program. The integrity of the insurance agent who advises you is as important as the soundness of the company from which you buy insurance. An insurance program is highly important to a family; many factors must be taken into consideration in developing such a program. Total expenditures for insurance should be in keeping with a person's income. Ordinarily, expenditures for insurance should increase as income increases. A life insurance program may be so planned as to provide income to meet emergencies and income when the earning period of life has passed.

CHAPTER 15

HOUSING THE FAMILY

You have followed the instructions in the previous chapters of this book. You have spent wisely and you have used a budget to help you to save. You have even invested some of your savings in some investment projects, and you have arranged for protection through insurance. By following a practical and realistic approach, you have amassed a fair amount of money. It's time to consider housing for the family.

SHOULD YOU BUY OR RENT A HOME?

Every family must have housing. You can buy a house, an apartment or a condominium; you can rent a house or an apartment, or you can build a house. You must decide which alternative to choose and how to finance the housing once you have made a choice. In this chapter, we analyze the factors that you should consider in making decisions about housing. For most people, housing is the largest personal expenditure that they will ever make. The comfort and satisfaction derived from housing is a matter of great importance. It is important that wisdom be exercised when purchasing a house.

Advantages and Disadvantages of Owning a Home

You should consider buying a house if:

a) You can finance ownership out of savings or by monthly payments out of current income
b) You expect to continue to live in the same area
c) You will derive more pleasure and satisfaction from owning than from renting.

Homeownership places certain responsibilities upon the members of the family. Usually, these responsibilities for financing, care and maintenance, and improving physical conditions and appearance are beneficial to you and your family, assuming that such responsibilities help individual members of the family to have a sense of pride and of participation in family affairs.

In as much as owning a home may seem to be a desirable objective, it may be economically unwise to buy or to build a house. For example, if you expect to move soon to another town, if property values are declining, if you don't have sufficient funds to make the necessary down payment, or if there is any likelihood that you will not be able to make the payments, buying a home would be an unwise decision. You should carefully calculate all the costs of owning a home and you should then consider them in the family budget. There are many who have neglected this wise counsel and have entered into home ownership without first counting the cost. The result is often embarrassment and considerable financial loss when foreclosure ensues.

The advantages and disadvantages of homeownership are summarized in the following table.

Table 15.1
Advantages and Disadvantages of Home Ownership

Advantage	Disadvantages
1. Home ownership gives a sense of security, and practically assures a home in old age. 2. Home ownership forces the establishment of a plan of saving. Payments beyond the cost of maintenance and ownership constitute savings. 3. Home ownership adds to individual and family prestige and improves credit rating, provided payments are made as scheduled. 4. Home ownership is a source of enjoyment, satisfaction, and pride.	1. The owner's equity or investment in the house is not readily available for use in making other expenditures. 2. The homeowner must assume responsibility for financing, maintenance, and improvements. 3. Home ownership makes moving from one community or city to another difficult. 4. During the period of making payments, home ownership may require larger monthly expenditures than renting. 5. Owning a home places upon the owner responsibilities for maintenance and repairs, such as painting, lawn care, and snow removal.

Housing Options

A family often must decide whether it should buy a new house, buy an old house, or build its own home. Most families do not have the amount of money required to purchase their "dream" home. It is often necessary, therefore, to make certain choices to get the most satisfactory home for the funds that are available. Very often, an entirely new home will cost more than an old home for the same housing amenities. However, a newly built home will probably cost less for repairs over a number of years. On the other hand, some old homes that are in excellent condition may be better buys than new homes. There is another important factor in buying an old home. It is often necessary to remodel or repair the old house before moving in. It may need a new roof, a new furnace, or other types of repairs. Sometimes an additional room must be added. These costs must all be taken into consideration in fitting the cash outlay into the budget. A new home may hold its value better than an old home, but in either case, it is well to consult a reliable person who can help you judge the value. Appraisals that are made in attempting to obtain a loan will usually help to determine value.

If you intend to build a home, you should consider the following five choices:

1. Engage the complete services of an architect.
2. Engage the limited services of an architect, providing him or her with stock plans—pre-drawn plans ordered from a supplier through a catalogue or a web site.
3. Engage a contractor, using stock plans.
4. Buy stock plans and arrange with several contractors for different parts of construction.
5. Buy a prefabricated house and engage a builder to erect it.

In some cases, it is possible to engage the services of an architect on a limited basis by submitting to him or her stock or ready-made plans and asking him or her to make certain alterations. Another option is buying a prefabricated home. This sometimes saves some of the cost of building. If you have the ability, you can do some of the construction yourself; but generally it is desirable to engage a competent builder to do at least the main part of the work.

Selecting a Home

The location of the home is important. You will face two main problems when buying a home. The first problem is to select the right place to live. Satisfactory answers should be provided to such questions as: Are schools and shopping areas near? Are adequate police and fire protection provided? Are such residential improvements as good streets, sidewalks, and utilities provided? The second problem is to select the right house. Some things to consider are style, construction, amount of yard space, adequate insulation, condition of electrical wiring and plumbing, adequate room size and storage facilities, and heating plant.

Some communities are improving; some are well established; some new communities are difficult to judge as to their future development; some are declining because property is deteriorating, factories are moving in, and people are moving into better areas.

When to Buy a Home

Under normal circumstances, the best time to buy a home is *not* when prices of real estate are high; but on the other hand, this is usually the time when the family has its greatest income and is able to save enough money to make a substantial down payment. Therefore, the answer to when a family should buy a home is determined largely by the following factors:

1. Whether or not the family has enough money saved to make a substantial down payment.
2. Whether or not future income is reasonably assured so that the monthly payments can be continued with a margin of safety.
3. Whether or not future income will provide for additional funds over and above monthly payments to pay for insurance

premiums, property taxes, and property improvements that arise each year.

Paying for the Home

All authorities in home management, financing, and home building insist that no family should buy a home until a very careful budget plan has been worked out. After shopping in a desirable location for a home that will take care of the family for several years, you should prepare a budget that takes into consideration the down payment and all the carrying and operating charges, including the monthly payments.

Paying Cash

Buying a house for cash may seem desirable. However, if you buy a house for cash, you should not invest so much that you must use all the funds that you have laid aside for use in an emergency. For instance, if you use all your cash to purchase a house, you may not have any reserve in case of a serious illness or some other emergency. If you acquire a house by means of borrowed money, you make a serious mistake if you buy beyond your capacity to pay the interest charge and to repay the loan.

If the loan is too great, you may become discouraged because of the need of cutting down the level of living and thus depriving your family of those things required to maintain health. You may even lose the house through foreclosure proccedings.

In buying a house, many young people gamble to the extent of assuming that their earnings will increase. They, therefore, undertake a greater obligation than they should. Discouragement then results if future earnings do not become greater, or if they become less.

Cost of Home and Annual Income

The amount that you may spend for the interest and principal on a home is always an issue. Builders, realtors, and lenders of money estimate that between 20 and 25 percent of the assured income of a family may safely be spent in buying a home. This should include interest, amount of principal, taxes, and insurance.

If you have been renting a house and you decide to buy it, you may be faced with greater expenses than those required in renting. If it has not been possible for you to save money while renting, it will probably not be possible for you to finance the purchase of a home. Some people do, however, undertake such a purchase because they are then forced to follow some definite plan of saving.

The Down Payment

The purchase of a home can be financed in many ways, but usually, the buyer must pay part of the original price in cash. Of course, the lending institution states the amount of down payment that it considers necessary as partial protection for the loan. In some jurisdictions, governments, through specific agencies, develop plans for minimum down payment. These usually range from 5 to 20 percent. Many financial consultants, however, recommend that a person who finances the purchase of a home on a time basis should make a cash down payment of at least 20 percent of the purchase price.

The Monthly Payment

Lenders today generally provide mortgages on the basis of monthly payments. It follows then that a critical factor that you should consider when purchasing a home is the monthly payments. You should be reasonably sure that you have sufficient income to be able to meet the monthly payments. Your budgeting activity should help to determine whether you are able to meet this financial obligation. The amount of the monthly payment should be sufficient to reduce insurance, taxes, principal, and interest.

Other Costs to Consider

The down payment and the monthly payments are not the only costs to consider when purchasing a home. Other costs to consider include items such as floor covering, curtains and drapes, and landscaping including lawn and trees. You could very well be surprised if you do not plan for these expenses.

The Canadian Imperial Bank of Commerce (CIBC) suggests a number of additional costs that you may have to pay. They are summarized in the following table. These cost estimates will have to be adjusted to suit the particular circumstances.

Table 15.2
Additional Costs Involved in Buying a New Home (2017)

Item	Approximate cost
Property valuation fee	$150-$200
Home inspection fee	$500
Property survey	$750-$1,000
Land transfer tax	$5,700
Legal fees	$1,300-$2,500
Title insurance	$250
Prepaid property tax and utility adjustments	$400-$500
Home insurance	$450/year

Source: https://www.cibc.com/en/personal-banking/mortgages/resource-centre/add-costs-when-buying-home.html

The Buy or Rent Decision

I have often been asked whether it is better to buy or rent when it comes to housing. It is an important question; but there are many occasions when the only option available to many young families, or even older ones, is renting. That is the case, for example, if they cannot afford the down payment and additional costs of owning a home, or if they will be living in a given community only temporarily.

Owning or Renting—A Comparison

Many *personal* factors enter into the buying or renting decision, but we can point out some factors that you should consider when making the decision. There are costs and benefits, and advantages and disadvantages to consider in each case. In the following series of tables, we provide useful information to help you decide whether to rent or buy a home.

Table 15.3
Cost of Buying versus Renting

Cost of Buying	Cost of Renting
Down payment	Monthly rent
Insurance	Utilities
Property taxes	Moving costs
Utilities	First month's rent
Home appraisal	Security deposit.
Loan (Mortgage) payment	
Home inspection	
Moving costs	
Maintenance and repairs	
Home improvement.	

Table 15.4
Advantages of Buying versus Renting

Advantages of Buying	Advantages of Renting
Freedom to do as you wish with the home	Easier to relocate
Equity	No responsibility for maintenance & repairs
Pride of home ownership	Not affected by declining real estate values.
Certain tax benefits offered to homeowners.	

Table 15.5
Disadvantages of Buying versus Renting

Disadvantages of Buying	Disadvantages of Renting
High upfront costs	No tax benefits for home ownership
Loss from property devaluation	No equity build up
Responsibility for maintenance and repairs.	Limited security of housing
	Landlords, not you, have control over the rent.

Be Cautious in Buying

If you decide a buy a home, make sure there is room in the budget to maneuver. Costs can change. For example, interest rates on your mortgage can increase. To be safe, you should try to make a substantial down payment. This will reduce the amount of the monthly payments.

Chapter Summary

Whether you should buy or rent a home depends on your particular circumstances. There are important facts to investigate when deciding to buy or rent a home. A budget will help you determine whether or not you can afford to buy a home. A down payment of at least 20% is usually recommended. Whether you are buying or renting a home, the location should be given due consideration. A mortgage is a contract between the buyer of the property and the lender of the funds. An appraisal of the property is both necessary and desirable.

APPENDIX

GLOSSARY OF FINANCIAL TERMS

A

Advertisement: a paid public announcement promoting a product, service, or event, using television, radio, posters, and other media.

Annuity: a contract typically between an individual and an insurance company in which the individual pays a lump sum of money in return for a stream of regular payments in the future.

Asset: something of value that someone owns.

B

Balance sheet: a statement of assets, liabilities, and owners' equity.

Balloon payment: a final large payment to liquidate a loan after a series of regular smaller timely payments.

Bank: a financial institution that accepts deposits from the public, makes loans to borrowers and offers other financial services to its customers.

Bond: an official paper document given by a borrower such as a government or a private corporation (called the issuer) promising to pay a stipulated rate of interest during the life of the bond to repay the principal when the bond matures.

Budget: a financial plan outlining an entity's expected income, expected expenditures, and planned savings for a given period.

Buying power: the amount of goods and services that a given sum of money can buy. Also called purchasing power.

C

Capital: money invested in a business and may include assets such as cash, machinery, and buildings.

Cash: bank notes and coins.

Certificate of deposit (CD): a savings instrument given by a financial institution with a fixed interest rate and a fixed maturity date.

Checking account: an account at a bank that allows you to transfer funds by writing checks.

Collateral: an asset that serves as security for a loan. The item is taken if the loan is not repaid.

Compound interest: interest that is paid both on the principal and on the accumulated interest.

Cost: the amount of money paid to acquire an item.

Credit (noun): the ability to obtain goods, services, or money now with a promise to pay at a later date.

Credit (verb): to obtain goods, services, or money now with a promise to pay in the future.

Credit card: a card made of plastic issued by a business that you can use to obtain goods and services now and pay for them in the future.

Credit union: a not-for-profit financial institution that accepts deposits, makes loans, and provides a wide array of other financial services and products.

Creditworthy: sufficiently sound, financially, to merit the extension of credit.

Cryptocurrency: a type of digital currency that allows people to make payments directly to each other through an online system.

D

Debenture: a type of debt instrument issued by companies to raise funds. A debenture is not secured by physical assets.

Debit (noun): an entry indicating something one owes.

Debit (verb): to subtract money from one's account.

Debt: money or other obligation that one owes to an individual, business, or government.

Depository institution: a financial institution such as a bank or credit union that accepts checking or saving deposits.

Direct deposit: money sent electronically to one's account at a financial institution.

Dividend: a portion of a company's profits that is paid out to its shareholders.

E

Electronic funds transfer (EFT): the transfer of money electronically from one bank account to another.

Entrepreneur: one who organizes, manages, and assumes the risks of a business.

Equity: the difference between assets and liabilities.

Estate: the money and property owned by someone.

Exchange rate: the rate at which one currency exchanges for another currency.

F

Financial institution: an institution such as a bank or credit union that offers financial services.

Fixed expenses: payments whose values are constant and generally known in advance like rent.

Foreclosure: an action of taking possession of a property for failure to make payments as agreed.

G

Generational wealth: wealth handed down from one generation to another.

Grace period: the number of days you have to pay a bill before finance charges begin.

Gross income: total income before any deductions are made.

H

Health insurance: an agreement in which an insurance company agrees to pay for some or all of your medical expenses in exchange for a monthly premium payment.

Homeowner's insurance: a form of property insurance that covers losses and damages to your residence, along with furnishings and other assets in the home.

I

Impulse buying: buying things that you did not plan to buy.

Inflation: a persistent increase in the average level of prices over time.

Insurance: a means of protection from financial loss in which, in exchange for a fee, a party agrees to compensate another party in the event of certain loss, damage, or injury.

Interest: a fee paid by a lender to a borrower for the use of money.

Interest rate: the amount a lender charges a borrower expressed as a percentage of the amount borrowed.

Investment: something you buy with the expectation of earning a financial return in the future.

L

Lease: a legal agreement by which the owner of a building, a piece of land, or something such as a car allows someone else to use it for a period of time in return for money.

Liability: something one owes; a debt.

Liquid asset: an asset that can easily be converted into cash without much loss

Liquidity: a measure of the ease with which one can access money.

Loan: money lent or borrowed usually to be repaid with interest.

M

Maturity date: the date on which the final payment of a debt obligation becomes due.

Money: anything that is generally acceptable as payment for goods and services or in the settlement of a debt.

Mortgage: a type of loan used to purchase or maintain a home, plot of land, or other types of real estate.

Mutual fund: a company that pools money from many investors and invests the money in securities such as stocks, bonds, and short-term debt.

P

Policy (insurance): a written contract between the insured and the insurer outlining the type of protection provided and the amount of money to be paid by the insured.

Premium: the amount of money that has to be paid for insurance coverage.

Principal: the original sum of money invested, lent, or borrowed.

Profit: the difference between what you sell something for and what it costs to acquire it.

Property tax: a tax on property usually houses and land.

R

Rate of return: the return (profit or loss) on an investment expressed as a percentage of the amount invested.

Return: the profit or loss on an investment.

Risk: exposure to loss, harm, or danger.

S

Savings: the amount of money set aside for future use.

Savings account: an account at a financial institution in which you deposit funds for which interest is paid.

Savings goal: the amount of money you plan to save for a specific purpose by a stipulated time.

Security: an investment instrument such as a stock or bond.

Stock: an investment instrument that gives you part ownership in a company.

T

Taxes: mandatory payments levied by governments on individuals and businesses to finance their operations.

Transaction fee: a fee that is charged by a credit card company each time the card is used for certain transactions.

V

Variable expenses: expenses that change from month to month.

W

Wage: compensation for labour services.

Will: a legal document specifying a person's wish regarding the disposal of his/her estate after death.

www.ingramcontent.com/pod-product-compliance
Lightning Source LLC
Chambersburg PA
CBHW061736070526
44585CB00024B/2702